Swarthmore Lecture 1969

BEARINGS
OR FRIENDS AND THE
NEW REFORMATION

by Maurice A. Creasey

Friends Home Service Committee
Friends House   Euston Road   London N.W.1

First Published May 1969

Cover design by John Blamires
Printed in Great Britain in 10/12 Times
By Headley Brothers Ltd., 109 Kingsway, London, W.C.2
and Ashford, Kent.

PREFACE

The Swarthmore Lectureship was established by the Woodbrooke Extension Committee at a meeting held December 9th, 1907 ; the minute of the Committee providing for 'an annual lecture on some subject relating to the message and work of the Society of Friends'. The name Swarthmore was chosen in memory of the home of Margaret Fox, which was always open to the earnest seeker after Truth, and from which loving words of sympathy and substantial material help were sent to fellow workers.

The Lecturer alone is responsible for any opinions expressed.

The Lectures have usually been delivered at the time of the assembly of London Yearly Meeting of the Society of Friends. The present Lecture, in abridged form, was delivered at Friends House, Euston Road, on the evening of May 30th, 1969.

In 1966 the Friends Home Service Committee took over the publication of the Swarthmore Lectures from George Allen & Unwin Ltd., who had published them for many years.

CONTENTS

INTRODUCTION

'Why "bearings"? And what do you mean by the "New Reformation"?' These two questions arose immediately, I am sure, in the minds of many Friends when they learned the title of this year's Swarthmore Lecture. So I want to begin by suggesting brief answers to them, answers which the rest of this book will have to expand and develop.

We all know that the decade which is now ending has been a time of flux and ferment, of radical questioning and widespread unsettlement in matters of belief and conduct. It has also been a time of unprecedented stirrings and experiments affecting the faith and the structure of even the largest Christian communion, the Roman Catholic church, hitherto thought of as the very symbol of changelessness.

In the minds of a good many people credit—or blame—for much of this unsettlement came to be attached to John Robinson, whose book *Honest to God*[1] brought to millions some inkling of what had previously been discussed only in academic circles or among small, consciously radical groups of churchmen. It was, in fact, a somewhat later book of his[2] which gave general currency to the term 'new Reformation' as a possible description of this contemporary ferment. But these books were but two of a much greater number, many of them published in paperback editions, which opened up for discussion, often in a quite radical and uninhibited manner, every aspect of Christian—indeed, any theistic—faith, challenged practically every ethical principle and questioned every traditional form of the church's life, whether doctrinal, devotional or institutional. So, when I speak of the new Reformation I am referring to all the attitudes and protests

[1] Robinson (John) *Honest to God*. London: SCM, 1963.
[2] Robinson (John) *The New Reformation?* London: SCM, 1965.

1

and programmes which have been finding expression in such books. These are now the subject of frequent and concerned discussion not only in the religious but also in the secular press. They are also matters which, whenever Friends meet, whether for worship or for conference, underlie a good deal of what is actually said and perhaps colour even more of what is thought.

Now, when I let my imagination play around all this, I find myself picturing the matters dealt with in these books as being like a chain of islands standing out of the sea of contemporary life. On the surface they are all separate from one another, but below the surface they are connected. They mark underwater ridges and reefs, the strata of which are exposed in them for our examination. Around them swirl currents, and against them dash breakers. But they give hospitality to a variety of living things which, apart from them, would be homeless. And from time to time they offer shelter, even if only temporary, for castaways whose traditional faith has been dashed to pieces in the surf, or who have been swept by mysterious currents away from the frequented ocean lanes. There they find themselves—and one another.

It should now be clear, I think, from this nautical excursion, why the theme of the new Reformation suggested to me the idea of 'bearings'. It seems to me that it may be timely for us as Friends to 'take our bearings' on these 'islands', to judge our position in relation to them, to assess how far we can allow ourselves to be carried forward by the currents which sweep around them and how far we need to bestir ourselves to strenuous navigation. Doubtless my mind was predisposed to think in such pictorial terms by the title which was given to one of the more significant of these books. In his introduction, its editor speaks of the present as 'a time for soundings, not charts or maps'.[3] It is certainly not my intention to offer

[3] Vidler (A. R.) ed. *Soundings*. Cambridge: University Press, 1962, p. ix.

2

detailed maps. But I believe it is both desirable and possible at this time to gain some general idea of the directions in which we need to move, the points towards which we should steer, the areas in which we may expect to encounter hazardous cross-currents or become enveloped in fog more dense than that in which we are used to navigating.

Looking back over the series of some sixty Swarthmore Lectures, I find that the one which is closest to my own in purpose and scope is the Lecture for the year 1920 entitled *Quakerism and the future of the Church*,[4] given by my beloved and revered predecessor at Woodbrooke, Herbert G. Wood. To him I feel I owe any insight I may have into the meaning of Christian faith and discipleship as these have been known among Friends. Through him, also, I have come to feel a deep concern that the truth as Friends have known it may be ever more vitally related both to whatever has proved its truth in the experience of men everywhere and also to the ongoing apprehension by the Christian fellowship as a whole of the truth as it is in Jesus.

In relation to the theme of the new Reformation, that Lecture, given in the shadow of the First World War, is notable in at least three respects. It recognised that even then, half a century ago, the churches were seen by 'the great bulk of Englishmen' as 'irrelevant to the actual practical tasks of the day'.[5] But it also claimed that it was 'their very response to elements in Christianity which makes men dissatisfied with the churches'. Furthermore, it recognised that it was nothing less than the continued existence of 'organised Christianity' that was in doubt, and the question was explicitly raised 'Have the churches with which we are familiar any prospect of outriding the

[4] Wood (H. G.) *Quakerism and the future of the Church*. London: Swarthmore Press, 1920.
[5] Wood, *op. cit.*, p. 12.

present storm?'[6] In several places H. G. Wood expressed his belief that 'one great weakness of the churches at the present time is that we are still groping after a theology which is at once simple and profound, loyal to the historic revelation and loyal to the manifestations of truth in modern science—a theology which could interpret life's meaning and purpose as clearly as Calvinism used to do or as Marxism does—a theology which will satisfy the mind and stir the heart—a theology that can be preached'.[7]

Not only did the lecturer thus describe the need of the hour as being for a comprehensive theological framework having about it the 'clearness and the force which comes from a luminous regulative idea', comparable to Calvinism or Marxism—a view rarely expressed nowadays—but he even felt able to express the belief that 'the outlines of a new theology are probably lying to our hand'.[8] He indicated the kind of theology he had in mind when he said, 'We have the elements of a new and better theology in the work of teachers like Erskine and McLeod Campbell'.[9] And he felt able to make the claim that 'much that is vital in modern theology is essentially the reaffirmation of the Quaker faith in a universal inward saving light'. He continued: 'There is hardly a significant movement in modern theology which does not in some way re-illumine and develop some aspect of this central Quaker contention.' He traced the origins of this movement in modern theology to Schleiermacher, its influence on English theology to Coleridge and its further development to Ritschl. But, contrary to the opinions of F. D. Maurice and Thomas Hancock, H. G. Wood believed that 'the religious progress of the last century' had not 'rendered the Society of Friends superfluous'.

[6] Wood, *op. cit.*, p. 7.
[7] *Ibid.*, p. 29.
[8] *Ibid.*, p. 49.
[9] *Ibid.*, p. 29.

4

'The whole Christian community,' he claimed, 'still needs the witness of a corporate body like the Society of Friends to the Quaker type of sainthood, to the value of silence, to the true nature of Christian democracy, and to the paramount claims of positive goodwill on Christian thought and effort.'[10]

The significance of the Swarthmore Lecture for 1920 in relation to our present theme seems to me to be this. Here was one of the most penetrating and capacious minds to which the Society has given a home in this present century striving to discern the future of the church and of the Society of Friends in relation to it. He saw clearly and felt keenly the widespread sense of the church's irrelevance to the problems of social and political life. He was prepared to face the possibility that all the existing structures of the churches might have to be radically changed and even discarded. But he remained serenely confident both that 'the Christian fellowship will never be blotted out'[11] and also that the characteristic witness of the Society of Friends had still a vital part to play in the upbuilding and maintenance of that fellowship. He saw the pressing need for a comprehensive and yet profoundly simple statement of the Christian faith rooted in experience and manifesting itself in an infectious joy and strength. And he cherished the belief that, even as he spoke, the outline of such a statement, reflecting at many points the emphases which had always been central to Quakerism, was being prepared and would receive general acceptance. He was no less clear that the churches must move towards 'a genuine Catholic unity',[12] recognising that 'all churches are imperfect and incomplete, that the one body of Christ is outwardly divided'. Characteristically, however, he realised that 'to all the churches comes the question: Have you

[10] Wood, *op. cit.*, pp. 69-70.
[11] *Ibid.*, p. 8.
[12] *Ibid.*, p. 85.

any sure guidance to offer men in creating a true international, in recreating our industrial order?' And with his customary clearsightedness he noted the importance of observing that 'the pooling of our several inheritances will not necessarily equip the one Church for the tasks of today'. He ended his Lecture with this sober expression of his unshakeable conviction: 'If we are faithful we shall find ourselves asserting the same Christian values, preaching the same Gospel. We shall enter into a new comradeship of co-operation. Through the breakdown of the old order, Christ may reunite His Church and further the redemption of humanity.'[13]

The questions which press themselves unrelentingly upon me, and to which in this present lecture I am struggling to find answers, are these. Standing, as I believe I do, in the same fundamental faith and experience as H. G. Wood, can I today, amidst the radical questioning not only of 'the churches' and of 'organised religion' but even of 'God' and 'religion' itself, still assert the necessity and possibility of a clear, simple, profound statement of the Christian faith organised around a single, luminous idea? And, if I can, can I also claim that the Society of Friends still has a vocation to exemplify and witness to that idea? Must I, too, affirm my belief in the necessity, for the foreseeable future, of the continuing separate existence of the Society of Friends? And if I do not, what do I propose instead? And what is to be said about the marked diversities within the Society?—a fact of which, today, after four World Conferences of Friends, there is a much more general awareness than there was in 1920.

Having spoken thus personally of the standpoint from which I feel bound to approach the questions with which this lecture will deal, I want to conclude this introduction by setting out, in outline, the argument which the rest of the lecture will develop.

[13] Wood, *op. cit.*, p. 86.

6

In recent years it has seemed to me increasingly clear that the various Christian denominations can best be understood as offering different types of answer to a series of questions raised in a pointed form by the Reformation of the sixteenth and seventeenth centuries. But between us and that 'old Reformation' lies a great divide, or a great transition, constituted by an immeasurably profound change in our knowledge of our environment and an unprecedentedly rapid extension of our power over it. It is now coming to be generally realised that in this situation we all, whatever our denominational standpoints, are being confronted by an altogether new series of questions, questions which were not, and could not have been, the concern of the Reformers. The great question, therefore, facing all the churches, as it seems to me, is whether they are to continue to be preoccupied with the frame of reference resulting from the old Reformation, or with the frame of reference constituted by the new Reformation amidst the upheavals and unsettlements of which we are now living. An ecumenical movement which, even if successful, sought only to unite Christian churches on the basis of the old frame of reference, would be, in my judgement, stillborn. But an ecumenical movement which, while not ignoring the older questions, concentrated upon the new, would be both full of promise and would also call for radical re-examination on the part of all the churches of their basic beliefs, attitudes and structures.

But what is true among the churches is also true within each of them. This applies, I believe, as truly to the Society of Friends as to any other Christian communion. There is within the Society, as we all know, marked diversity of religious belief, attitude and structure. What is also increasingly clearly shown in the series of World Conferences and in the existence and growing importance of the Friends' World Committee for Consultation, is a deep desire, within all branches of the

Society, for greater mutual comprehension, co-operation and unity. But what is, perhaps, less clearly understood is that these diversities within the Society are, like those among the churches, related to a religious and theological background which is more and more coming to be seen as antiquated. Therefore a 'solution' of the Society's internal ecumenical problem which was related only to that old background would be sterile. The only unity worth striving for, whether among the churches or within the Society of Friends, is a unity which rests upon a radical and profound reapprehension, in contemporary terms, of what I will call, in a phrase the meaning of which will, I hope, become clearer as we proceed, *the fullness of Christ for the wholeness of man.*

As best I can within the limits of this lecture, I want to amplify this argument by looking first in Chapter One at the new frame of reference, the contemporary questions in theology to which anything we say must be related if it is to be judged worth listening to. Then, in Chapter Two, I want to try to show why these particular questions have emerged with such force just now, in the second half of the twentieth century. This will lead me in Chapter Three to offer some general comments by way of critical appraisal of this contemporary frame of reference, for nothing is to be assumed to be true simply because it is new. Finally, in Chapter Four, I shall try to bring all this together into a closer relation to our own special interests and concerns as Friends, and to suggest the bearings by which our course in the coming decades is to be set.

I

THE NEW REFORMATION—WHAT IS IT?

A few pages back, I pictured the books in which the new Reformation has found expression in the past decade as a chain of islands upon whose positions we, as Friends, need to 'take bearings'. I now want to take up the other aspect of the simile, and to speak rather in terms of a geological survey of this chain of islands. I am going to suggest that there are to be found exposed more or less fully on most of them four strata or formations.

There is first the stratum of theology—the 'radical' or, as it is often called in a daringly paradoxical phrase, the 'death-of-God' theology. Next, there is a layer of concern for a radically new understanding of the world, particularly in its contemporary phase of 'secularity' and 'religionlessness'. Thirdly, there is a preoccupation with ethical questions, expressed frequently in such phrases as 'the new morality' and 'situational ethics'. Lastly, there is a remarkable concentration of attention upon the church, both from the point of view of its institutional structures and also with reference to the relations among its historical forms.

Within the limits of a small book, this survey will have to be an aerial one rather than a detailed going over the ground on foot, hammer in hand, so to speak. But more detailed surveys exist in plenty, and I have indicated in the suggestions for further reading some of the most useful of them. In this chapter my purpose is, first, to invite attention to some of the more important general features of these four areas of discourse, features which may indeed even be missed by those who only have an eye for detail. In the next chapter, I want to try to account for the fact that these concerns have emerged in this form and in such relation to one another at this particular time.

The 'radical theology'

I can, perhaps, best indicate what he called 'the shape of the radical theology' by quoting from an article with that title written by William Hamilton, one of its leading exponents.[14] He describes it in terms of three 'motifs'. The first is the affirmation of the death of God. This metaphor describes 'something that is happening to a particular group of modern Western Christians'. It is, he claims, a better metaphor than the 'absence' or 'disappearance' or 'eclipse' of God, for it denotes 'a real loss, something irretrievable . . . exactly what we feel needs to be said'. The second motif is 'obedience to Jesus'. Hamilton is very well aware of the 'hosts of problems' which can be raised in connection with 'this godless Christology'. Chief among them is the obvious question 'Why have you chosen *Jesus* . . . and not Albert Camus, Martin Luther King or Francis of Assisi?' To this his own answer is: 'Jesus is the one to whom I repair, the one before whom I stand, the one whose way with others is also to be my way because there is something there, in his words, his life, his way with others, his death, that I do not find elsewhere.' The third motif Hamilton describes as 'optimism'. By this he means not insensitivity, nor any belief in the inevitability of progress, but a desire to 'say Yes to the world of rapid change, new technologies and the mass media'. He finds the firmest grounds for such optimism in the spectacle of 'today's Negro revolution' and in the widespread concern, often expressed by younger people through voluntary service, for the underprivileged and the deprived.

Because of the striking phrase in which the radical theology's

[14] Hamilton (William) The Shape of the Radical Theology. *The Christian Century*, October 6, 1965, pp. 1219-22.

first motif is expressed, 'radical' and 'death-of-God' theology have tended to become interchangeable terms. In addition to William Hamilton, two leading exponents of this type of theology who have caught the attention of many in the last five or six years are Paul van Buren and Thomas Altizer. All three are American, all are on the younger side of life, all are academic theologians or philosophers, and, so far as I know, all still affirm their right to be regarded as Christians. They have expressed their diverse, changing and developing views in books with such titles as *The Secular Meaning of the Gospel*,[15] *The New Essence of Christianity*[16] and, most striking of all, *The Gospel of Christian Atheism*.[17]

In a book entitled *Radical Theology and the Death of God*,[18] in which they collaborated, Hamilton and Altizer have set out no fewer than ten different senses in which the phrase 'death-of-God' is currently used or understood in discussions of the radical theology. There is, for example, the view that the death of God means simply the death of false or inadequate ideas of God. The view of traditional atheism, that there neither is nor ever has been any reality corresponding to the word God as used by religion, they mention only to reject. The sense in which they themselves use the phrase is that there was formerly a God to whom the appropriate response was worship, but that now there is no longer any such. The view which, in amplification of this, is expressed most clearly by Altizer, asserts that God, in the incarnation in Jesus Christ, emptied himself fully and finally of his transcendence, and in this sense being 'dead',

[15] van Buren (P.) *The Secular Meaning of the Gospel*. London, SCM, 1963.
[16] Hamilton (W.) *The New Essence of Christianity*. London: Darton, 1966.
[17] Altizer (T. J.) *The Gospel of Christian Atheism*. Philadelphia: Westminster Press, 1966.
[18] Hamilton (W.) and Altizer (T. J.) *Radical Theology and the Death of God*. Indianapolis: Bobbs-Merrill, 1966.

2

is now to be encountered only in his immanence in history and in our fellow men. But, in relation to the points to be discussed later, the view expressed in these words of Bonhoeffer is, perhaps, the most profound and suggestive form of the 'death-of-God' theology; 'God is teaching us that we must live as men who can get along very well without him. The God who is with us is the God who forsakes us . . . The God who makes us live in this world without using him as a working hypothesis is the God before whom we are ever standing.'[19] Here, clearly, we are confronted not by the 'death' but by the 'reticence' of God, that hiddenness which is the essential condition for our growth towards maturity.

From such a brief summary of what appear to be the more significant meanings of the phrase, one thing is already abundantly clear. It is a complete waste of time to discuss 'the death-of-God theology' with anyone until we are clear as to which meaning he intends. But it is scarcely less clear that, behind the various views of which I have given examples, there is a broad distinction between those who see the problem of a radical theology as being one of communication and those who see it as a problem of content. Is it a question of finding new ways of saying essentially the old things? Or is it a question of saying things that have never needed to be said before? Hamilton[20] himself clearly recognises that there are radicals of two types; he calls them 'soft' and 'hard' radicals. Of the former he says: 'They have the gospel, but they don't like the old words. They have God, but sometimes for strategic reasons they may decide not to talk about him.' But the 'hard' radicals, on the other hand, 'are really not interested in problems of communication . . . the message itself is problematic'. They

[19] Bonhoeffer (D.) *Letters and Papers from Prison.* London: SCM, 1953, p. 164.
[20] Hamilton (W.) The Shape of the Radical Theology. *The Christian Century*, October 6, 1965, pp. 1219-22.

'share first of all a common loss . . . not a loss of the idols, or of the God of theism. It is a loss of real transcendence. It is a loss of God.'

This distinction, which comes to sharp focus in the death-of-God debate, can be traced, also, through the other three areas of the new Reformation which will be discussed. In this wider setting we might well use the terms which William Hordern has suggested, 'translators' and 'transformers'.[21] The 'transformers', Hordern says, assume 'that the changes in the modern world have resulted in a qualitative transformation of man and his thinking'. Consequently, they believe that modern man 'can accept the Christian message only if it is changed drastically'. The 'translators', on the other hand, recognise that the world in which the Christian message has to be proclaimed and witnessed to is radically different in many important respects from any previous period in the world's history. But they do not therefore agree that the essentials of the faith must be changed or abandoned. It is along the line of this distinction that, as I see it, the main theological debate of the coming decades will be joined.

'Secularity'

'God and secularity: these are the poles between which the contemporary theological discussion moves.' These words of John Macquarrie[22] will serve to introduce the second of the four areas about which I wish to make some general descriptive comments.

The presence of these two poles was clearly recognised in William Hamilton's sketch of the shape of a radical theology. The same theologians for whom 'God' is a word of dubious

[21] Hordern (W.) in *New Directions in Theology Today*, Vol. I. Philadelphia: Westminster Press, 1966, pp. 142 ff.
[22] Macquarrie (John) in *New Directions in Theology Today*, Vol. III. Philadelphia: Westminster Press, 1967, p. 13.

meaning are much concerned to affirm the importance of this world, to adopt a positive attitude towards it and to see in secular life the field in which the attitudes of Jesus are to be given ever-new application.

It would, I think, be fair to say that there are almost as many different interpretations and emphases to be encountered in the discussions of secularity as we saw there were in the debate about the death-of-God theology. But I believe there would be a fairly general agreement among exponents of 'secular Christianity' on the points I now propose to indicate.

They would agree, in the first place, in thinking of secularity as characteristic of a stage or phase of human development when men turn their attention decisively away from 'gods' or even 'God', and concentrate it upon the natural world and upon secular affairs. It is thus a turning of attention from the divine to the human, from the eternal to the temporal, from the supernatural to the natural.

But, in the second place, this change in the focus of attention is seen as a mark of liberation and maturity, of man's 'coming of age'. He now no longer thinks of himself as responsible to and under the scrutiny of an all-powerful, all-seeing supernatural being. In his increasing knowledge of and control over his natural environment, he believes he finds a valid and sufficient framework for all his activities, spiritual as well as physical. In this setting, the meaning of 'religion', if indeed the word is still to be used, undergoes a radical change. Indeed, parallel with the paradox of 'Christian atheism', we encounter that of 'religionless Christianity'. In the earlier stages of history, 'religion' involved belief in the existence of a supernatural realm, of divine beings, and in the central importance for man's well-being of the rendering to them due worship and to their authorised priestly officials reverent obedience. But with the coming of secularity, man is set free from all this.

'Salvation' has come to mean learning and obeying the requirements of the natural order, and managing it for the general good of mankind. 'Religion' is indistinguishable from a responsible and concerned dealing with this world.

One consequence of this attitude is, of course, the increasing application to theology and ethics of the methods of enquiry and the criteria of empirical truth which have been developed with such astonishing success in men's dealings with the physical world. Nothing is to be received on authority whether of church or scripture or allegedly inspired teacher. Statements are to be held to be meaningful only if they can be tested by the methods appropriate to the sciences. 'Religious experience' is suspect as mere subjectivity; a sense of sin is to be explained in terms of childhood experience or of inescapable involvement in the guilt of social and political policies and actions of which one disapproves but about which one feels unable to do anything effective.

But along with these attitudes there goes a powerful emphasis upon the significance of the historical Jesus. The claims made concerning him by the Christian scriptures and the classical traditions of Christian theology may be discounted or denied. But he is nevertheless seen as putting upon us an inescapable ethical claim and providing us with a supremely powerful motivation for compassionate action in the world. He is supremely 'the man for others', and the only criterion of a secular Christian is that, like Jesus, he should be concerned for the wellbeing of all who are dispossessed or exploited.

Many of the exponents of 'secular Christianity' are, clearly, deeply influenced by the 'prison-epistles' of Dietrich Bonhoeffer, with their haunting questions and their undeveloped hints and suggestions which, despite all their apparent unconventionality, are usually deeply rooted in Biblical faith and piety. Some, indeed, argue that Bonhoeffer's

15

insights do no more than penetrate to the central meaning of the Hebrew-Biblical-Christian story. This tells how, in the purpose of God, first a tribe, then a nation and ultimately a fellowship transcending all national boundaries, has been liberated from superstitious dependence upon the cosmic order and liberated into the responsible freedom of sons of God.

Thus, by some, secularisation is regarded as the key to the meaning of world history.[23] By others secularisation is interpreted mainly in relation to the rise of urban, technological and industrial civilisation. Thus Harvey Cox, in his book *The Secular City*,[24] argues that 'Technopolis', the unimaginably vast and complex network of relations into which more and more of mankind is being drawn by technology, economics and communications, is pointing forward to and making real in a secular manner the prophetic vision of the kingdom of God being with men. In making such a claim, however, the negative aspects of Technopolis are not ignored. Thus, for example, we are reminded by Colin Williams[25] that 'wherever the promise is, there also the dangers gather', and that the marvels of modern technological society, while offering us 'an unprecedented power to subdue the earth', nevertheless offer also 'an unprecedented opportunity for atheistic self-assertion'.[26]

---

[23] This argument is developed, for example, by A. T. van Leeuwen in his book *Christianity in World History* (London: Edinburgh House, 1964), in which he attempts to show that the dynamic, world-embracing influence of western civilisation is the form in which the divine purpose to unify and transform all things is now entering upon a decisive stage. (cf. C. F. von Weizsacker's 1959-60 Gifford Lectures on *The Relevance of Science*. (London: Collins, 1964.)

[24] Cox (Harvey) *The Secular City*. London: SCM, 1966.

[25] Williams (Colin) *Faith in a Secular Age*. London: Collins (Fontana), 1966, p. 33.

[26] A similar point is strikingly made by E. R. Wickham, in his book *Encounter with Modern Society*. (London: Lutterworth, 1964, p. 28.) 'God says to the human race, wake up, grow up, get together . . . It is the logic of technology, whether you like it or not—waking up, growing up, getting together. It could spell heaven, it can certainly spell hell.'

Before I leave this subject, I should perhaps point out that a similar distinction is to be observed in the case of the 'secular Christians' as in that of the 'death-of-God theologians'. They range themselves into the categories of 'soft' and 'hard', 'translators' and 'transformers'. For the former, secularity is the form in which God's single, unbroken redemptive purpose is finding expression in our day, and for its understanding and proper utilisation it calls for a deeper understanding of the Christian faith. For the latter, however, secularisation marks the stage at which man is compelled to accept the full burden of responsibility for himself and for his world. He is 'on his own'—as, indeed, he always has been—but now, at last, he knows it. Only by being completely 'demythologized' into a statement of what is involved in authentic existence can the Hebrew-Christian religious tradition now speak to his condition.

'New morality' or 'Situational ethics'

If, as was said earlier, God and secularity are the two poles between which the contemporary theological discussion moves, we shall be prepared for the general effect of a discussion moving on the lines indicated in the previous two sections when it touches the field of morals. In so far as morality has been thought of by most people as involving obedience either to the commands of a divine transcendent law-giver or to the immanent principles of some kind of natural law, the contemporary death-of-God discussion and its setting in an anti-metaphysical framework clearly weaken the foundations of any such prescriptive morality. Similarly, with the increasing attention given to the pragmatic and empirical aspects of human experience, the growing recognition of the extent to which norms of conduct are shaped by social pressures, and the greater sensitivity now generally shown towards certain forms of injustice and exploitation, it is not to be wondered at that the ethical quality of any action will be assessed in terms of the extent to which love, interpreted as kindness or benevolence, finds expression through it. Speaking very generally, therefore, the 'new morality' or 'situational ethics' is to be seen as an understandable corollary of the theological positions expressed in the movement we are calling the 'new Reformation'.

Interestingly enough, the phrase 'the new morality' appears to have originated in Papal usage.[27] For most people in this country, however, it was probably the publication of *Soundings*[28] in 1962 and *Honest to God*[29] in the following year that placed this subject at the centre of general discussion and controversy. It may be worthwhile to point out that, although H. A. Williams' essay in *Soundings* on 'Theology and Self-awareness' and Bishop Robinson's sixth chapter entitled 'The New Morality' coincide at several points in their treatment of the norms of ethical judgment, these two pieces are really dealing with two distinct questions. H. A. Williams is concerned 'to discover how a man's knowledge of God and his attitudes towards God are affected by his growing awareness of what he is and how he functions as a psychic entity'.[30] In other words, he is seeking to use Freudian psychology to reinterpret Christian theology. Bishop Robinson, on the other hand, is aiming to demonstrate how acceptance of the 'radical theology'

[27] As long ago as 1952, Pope Pius XII, in an address to an international congress of the World Federation of Catholic Young Women, referred to the new ethical movement as 'ethical existentialism', sometimes known as a 'situationsethik'. In 1956, an Instruction of the Holy Office condemned 'the new morality' as contrary to Catholic doctrine. It was careful to make it clear that what was condemned was not 'the exercise of a proper prudence in the application of Natural Law to particular cases' but was 'a tendency to subordinate the objective moral law to some kind of subjective judgment which the individual claims to be immediate and decisive'.

[28] Vidler (A. R.) ed. *Soundings*. Cambridge: University Press, 1962.

[29] Robinson (John) *Honest to God*. London: SCM, 1963.

[30] Vidler (A. R.) ed. *Soundings*. Cambridge: University Press, 1962, p. 72.

involves a drastic reinterpretation of traditional moral judgments. Nevertheless, generally speaking, they coincide in their views of Christian ethics. Typical of the kind of statement which, understandably, caught public attention were these: 'Nothing can of itself always be labelled as wrong',[31] and 'Generous self-giving love is the ultimate moral value . . . This makes it impossible to describe certain actions as wicked and others as good. For only I myself can discover in what actions I am giving myself and in what actions I am refusing to give.'[32]

Perhaps the fairest way in which to describe very briefly the main features of situational ethics is to refer to its treatment by Joseph Fletcher who, in the English speaking countries, has come to be its main exponent. He seeks to develop a position distinguishable on the one hand from legalistic or prescriptive ethics and, on the other, from extemporism or illuminism. The 'starting question' for legalist ethics, Fletcher says, is 'What ought I to do?' For extemporist ethics it is 'What am I to do?' But for situational ethics it is 'What do I want?'[33] Throughout his writings, and most fully in his book from which I have just quoted, Fletcher sums up under six heads the position he is concerned to defend; they are as follows:

> 'Only one "thing" is intrinsically good; namely love: nothing else.'[34]
> 'The ruling norm of Christian decision is love: nothing else.'[35]
> 'Love and justice are the same, for justice is love distributed, nothing else.'[36]

[31] Robinson (John) *Honest to God*. London: SCM, 1963, p. 118.
[32] Vidler (A. R.) ed. *Soundings*. Cambridge: University Press, 1962, p. 80.
[33] Fletcher (J.) *Situation Ethics: The New Morality*. Philadelphia: Westminster Press, 1966, p. 42.
[34] *Ibid.*, p. 57.
[35] *Ibid.*, p. 69.
[36] *Ibid.*, p. 87.

'Love wills the neighbour's good whether we like him or not.'[37]

'Only the end justifies the means; nothing else.'[38]

'Love's decisions are made situationally, not prescriptively.'[39]

It is important to recognise that Fletcher does not wish to abolish all reference to principles or general rules. Thus he says of situational ethics that it brings together three things: 'Its one and only law, agape (love)'; the 'Sophia (wisdom) of the church and culture, containing many "general rules" of more or less reliability'; and 'the Kairos (moment of decision, the fullness of time) in which *the responsible self in the situation* decides whether the Sophia can serve love there or not' (Fletcher's italics). Of this summary Fletcher says: 'This is the situational strategy in capsule form.'[40] Elsewhere, he has said: 'Moral principles were made for men, not men for moral principles. That is situation ethics in a nut-shell.'[41]

Although I want to defer until later an attempt to form a critical estimate of this approach to ethical problems, it may be useful to take note of two considerations which help to put it into perspective. It has been pointed out (e.g. by G. F. Woods, in an essay on Situational Ethics)[42] that situational ethics exercises a wide appeal, for it can be accepted both by those who accept the 'death-of-God theology' and by those who do not. It is congenial both to existentialists of an atheistic kind, and also to secular humanists. It appeals to men who are

[37] Fletcher (J.) *Situation Ethics: The New Morality*. Philadelphia: Westminster Press, 19.6, p. 103.

[38] *Ibid.*, p. 120.

[39] *Ibid.*, p. 134.

[40] *Ibid.*, p. 33.

[41] Fletcher (J.) in *Storm over Ethics*. Philadelphia: United Church Press, 1967, pp. 169-70.

[42] Ramsey (Ian T.) ed. *Christian Ethics and Contemporary Philosophy*. London: SCM, 1966.

primarily concerned with practical affairs, and who know from painful experience how no two cases really come together under exactly the same categories. Its pragmatic and empirical emphases are attractive, furthermore, to those whose training is in the physical sciences. Remarkably enough, also, it has the sympathy of not a few Protestant theologians to whom the emphasis upon the 'I-thou' relationship with God mediated through the uniqueness of each situation of encounter is congenial.

But, if it exercises a wide appeal, it is nonetheless noticeable that the range of examples adduced by its leading exponents— and these include all three of the writers I have referred to—is remarkably restricted. With few exceptions, they are drawn from the most highly personal area of sex relations, and of situations in which ethical dilemmas of an exceptional and excruciatingly difficult kind are present. If it is true that hard cases make bad law, the same may also be true of ethics.

The structures and relationships of the churches

It may seem strange, at first sight, that, alongside of a rejection—or at any rate a radical questioning—of the traditional Christian concepts of God, a powerful new emphasis upon the meaning and value of the secular world and a radically situational approach to ethics, there should be taking place a great revival of interest in and concern for the church. Yet such is the case.

The aspect of this which probably springs first to the minds of most people is the ecumenical movement. The main Protestant traditions, stimulated by the pointed questions concerning the meaning of their inherited differences addressed to them by the so-called 'younger churches' of Africa and Asia, have, during the last sixty years, been carrying on a thorough collaborative examination both of their diversities and of their

21

common faith and loyalty. Regionally and locally more and more co-operation is now being accepted as natural and right. Old suspicions and competitiveness are being seen in their true light wherever collaboration in practical service, joint worship and sharing of resources become more general. Furthermore, alongside this world-wide movement of understanding and collaboration a few actual unions between churches have come into being already, and others are pending. During the present decade, this movement has been greatly extended by the growing participation of the Eastern Orthodox churches and, within limits, of the Roman Catholic church, a process which Pope John XXIII attributed to the initiative of the Holy Spirit and which the Second Vatican Council was able to translate to a remarkable extent not only into official pronouncements but also into a new spirit of 'ecumenism'.

It is, of course, possible to view this whole development from other points of view than that of Pope John. Some interpret it as simply a shortening of the lines, a getting together by the churches for mutual support in an indifferent or hostile world, to which what all the churches proclaim is increasingly irrelevant. It is fair to say, however, that many of those who are most concerned to make the churches relevant to the modern world owe their insight and concern to the ecumenical movement and are supporters of it.

Of these, many see not only the need for what is sometimes called a 'spiritual' unity among the churches but also a need for actual organic and visible unions. But they see also that these could be no more than marriages of the senile unless, at the same time, the churches were prepared to take a long hard look at themselves, at their beliefs, their ways of worship and their traditional structures, and were prepared also to make whatever changes in them were seen to be necessary. This point of view is forcefully expressed in John Robinson's second

22

paperback, *The New Reformation*[43] and in many other recent books.

At the roots of this contemporary concern for 'One Church Renewed for Mission' is a recovery, it is claimed, of an important New Testament insight regarding the nature and role of the church. The church is called to continue in the world Christ's work as Servant. Diverted from fulfilling this task by its acceptance of worldly power, authority and prestige throughout the 'Constantinian era' since the fourth century, the church must now abandon—indeed, is being compelled by the facts of history to abandon—all such pretensions. It must understand itself as 'the society in which the universal Kingship of God in Christ is acknowledged', as John Robinson has put it,[44] remembering all the time that Christ's Lordship is exercised through lowly service. It must move out into the world in which that Lordship is as yet unacknowledged. As the 'manifest church', in Tillich's phrase, its aim must be to address that 'latent church' hidden in the world, composed of men and women of all creeds and of none, who maybe unconsciously, are responding to the reconciling and healing purposes of God in the world. It must be able to offer itself to them as an 'accepting community', ready really to listen to their questions, prepared sometimes to raise with them new questions, and, above all, aiming to be a community in which salvation, in the sense of insight, healing and reconciliation is to be actually experienced and not merely talked about.

In order to fulfil such a role, it is argued, the churches must be prepared to make drastic changes in practically all their traditional structures. For, if heresy involves the distortion of the truth, there can be heretical structures just as really as there

[43] Robinson (John) *The New Reformation?* London: SCM, 1965.
[44] Robinson (John) *On being the Church in the World.* London: SCM, 1960, p. 20.

are heretical doctrines, structures which falsify the truths for which the churches claim to stand. Among such, as John Robinson and others argue, is the sharp traditional distinction between clergy and laity, leaders and led, shepherd and flock. Then there is the assumption that, for some people, service in and for the church should be regarded as a profession, carrying the right to permanent financial security. Least defensible of all, perhaps, is the tradition which, for most practical purposes, reserves leadership and authority within the churches to the male.

There are, it is argued, three areas in which such concerns for a new conception of the churches' role must find expression. There is, first, the area of urbanised and industrialised society in the developed countries. Here the churches have become peripheral to the lives and interests of the great majority. Here they must find radically new ways of working, breaking, maybe, both with the parish system and with the pattern of settled congregations in residential areas, and re-forming themselves in the places where people actually spend their working days. The churches must also cease being afraid to encourage their members to become so deeply involved in social, economic and political problems that they inevitably will run the risk of incurring criticism for 'interfering'; and the churches must be prepared to take a corporate stand on matters which involve clear issues of Christian principle and obedience.

The second area is that of taking fearless initiatives wherever men are being oppressed, exploited or deprived, and in urging upon governments and authorities the necessity of honouring their moral and legal obligations to all such. The third main area in which the contemporary concern with the church is finding expression is in relation to the world faiths. Here, on a world-wide scale, the churches are collaborating to set up and maintain Institutes for the sympathetic study, in depth, of

24

Buddhism, Hinduism and Islam, and to do this in frank and sincere co-operation with the intellectual and spiritual leaders of those faiths. Here too the aim is, not to convert or to proselytise but rather to discern and respond to what the divine purpose—or, as some would say, the Christ incognito— is effecting among men who do not call themselves by his name.

A by-product of the contemporary concern for the unity and relevance of the church is the growing recognition that, within the world-wide movement, there are growing up groups or families of churches which, sometimes to their own surprise and even embarrassment, are discovering specially close similarities of understanding and outlook. In so far as this process continues, the future of the ecumenical movement may well be concerned less with a large number of individual churches than with a small number of groups or families of churches, conscious among themselves of much closer unity than they feel towards the members of other groups or families of churches.

All this, and much more, is involved in what Bishop Robinson has described as the churches' need to 'live in the overlap', to maintain their own organic connexion with their own past and also to respond creatively to the startlingly new situations of today. He probably speaks for many who feel the strain and stress of the new Reformation when he says: 'Division and disintegration within each denomination, each local church, and indeed each Christian, produced by the strain of living in the overlap is an all too present possibility. Can the Church survive it? My faith is that it can—just.'[45]

---

[45] Robinson (John) *The New Reformation?* London, SCM, 1965, p. 99.

II

THE NEW REFORMATION—WHY NOW?

In the last chapter I have tried to make a general survey of the four 'strata', as I have called them, which are exposed in varying proportions and combinations in most of the books which I have pictured as 'islands' in the archipelago of the new Reformation. In this chapter, I want to try to answer the question, 'Why do these particular strata thrust themselves above the surface at just this point?' Or, to put the question less picturesquely, 'Why are these emphases being made *now*, at this particular time?'

I am not suggesting, of course, that nothing like these emphases has ever been made before. Anyone who will read John Macquarrie's brilliant analysis and critique in *Twentieth Century Religious Thought*,[46] or the same author's 'God and Secularity'[47] will recognise that all the emphases now being made, sometimes with a certain stridency and unguardedness, are developments of, or reactions to, tendencies which began to show themselves in the nineteenth and even in the eighteenth centuries.

Three things have to be understood about the new Reformation if we are to get our bearings realistically in relation to it. The first is that it has, I suggest, analogies with three previous periods in the history of Christian thought. Between the second and fourth centuries the church had to reckon with the change from a primitive to a Ptolemaic cosmology, and again in the sixteenth and seventeenth centuries the transition from a

[46] Macquarrie (John) *Twentieth Century Religious Thought*. London: SCM, 1963.

[47] Macquarrie (John) God and Secularity. *New Directions in Theology Today*, vol. 3. Philadelphia: Westminster Press, 1967, p. 13.

Ptolemaic to a Copernican and Newtonian cosmology. Then, again, in the mid-nineteenth century, with consequences vividly described by H. G. Wood in his *Belief and Unbelief since 1850*,[48] the Christian faith was compelled to come to terms with the new knowledge derived from the physical and biological sciences, and with the new vistas opened up by literary and historical criticism.

The second thing to be said is that we need to distinguish between what Professor T. F. Torrance has called 'the reformation that has been going on—largely unnoticed—since the early years of the century' and the 'rather crude and naïve notions' that have 'obtruded themselves vociferously upon this new Reformation'.[49] These two points taken together do not reduce the significance of the new Reformation movement as a whole, but only seek to guard against an uncritical assumption that it is all of a piece and has to be accepted whole or not at all, and that nothing remotely like it has ever occurred before.

But, this having been said, my third point must be to emphasise that, in a real sense, this contemporary ferment in religious thought is, in fact, unprecedented. It is unprecedented because, as I see it, it is a response to the unprecedented expansion in human knowledge and power which has occurred, for the most part, in living memory. It is in the twentieth century that the boundaries of our knowledge of the natural world have been pushed farther than in all the rest of human history put together. It is in the same period that our power to change and control our natural environment has increased more rapidly and more dramatically than in the whole of recorded history. These tremendous changes in the midst of which we are living have more remote causes which lie more than a

[48] Wood (H. G.) *Belief and Unbelief since 1850*. Cambridge: University Press, 1955.
[49] Torrance (T. F.) *Theology in Reconstruction*. London: SCM, 1963, p. 259.

3

thousand years back in history. Their more immediate causes are to be found from the seventeenth century onwards, when men became conscious of the possibilities of controlled and directed research and its applications to industry. But it is only in the last hundred years that this 'explosion' of knowledge and power and communications has begun obviously to shake the whole world, to change drastically the conditions of life for larger and larger numbers of human beings throughout the whole world. And not only to change their physical conditions of life. Even more importantly, it is revolutionising their whole understanding of the meaning and possibilities of life, so that they are no longer prepared to accept conditions which were only tolerable when they were thought to be inevitable. For the full deployment of these new powers and purposes, new social and political structures are seen to be necessary; education opens minds to hitherto undreamed of possibilities; fierce antagonisms develop between the forces of change and hope on the one hand and those of inertia or tradition or privilege on the other.

Now, it would indeed be incomprehensible if such vast and radical changes in men's knowledge and power and aspirations left unaffected their attitudes to religion, philosophy and ethics, the areas in which the broader and deeper significance of human life has hitherto been sought. It is the central thrust of my argument that what we are calling the new Reformation is to be understood as the reflection or counterpart in the fields of religion, philosophy and ethics of the latest and most dramatic phase of what Kenneth Boulding has called the 'great transition'.[50]

If we are right to relate the new Reformation in this way to the latest phase of the 'great transition', we are given a standpoint from which we may gain, I believe, a clearer understand-

[50] Boulding (Kenneth) *The Meaning of the Twentieth Century*. New York: Harper & Row, 1964.

28

ing of the relation between the 'old' Reformation and the 'new'. For an obvious and undeniable fact about the Reformation of the sixteenth century is that it lies on the other side of this phase of the 'great transition'. Despite its close association with that earlier phase which we call the Renaissance, the fact is that the Reformation was still to a very large extent medieval in outlook, sympathies and presuppositions. The main lines of the medieval world view, the medieval assumptions regarding human life and destiny, the medieval conception of the church's authority and of its relations with the secular power, the need for uniformity and the right of coercion in matters of religion—all these were not really questioned by the main Reformed churches. In them, too, in the seventeenth century, despite the vigorous stirrings of the new scientific spirit in the world around them, there developed in regard to doctrine a Protestant scholasticism less liberal and open minded even than some of the great medieval schoolmen.

At this point I am inclined to take up my nautical parable again. But this time it is to take seriously the traditional figure of the church as a ship, or, if we are to take account of the schism between the Eastern and Western forms of the church, as two ships! The Reformation of the sixteenth century, broadly speaking, left the ship of the Orthodox churches virtually untouched. For the ship of the Roman church, however, the Reformation and counter-Reformation involved a pretty thorough overhaul and refit; we might even add that it also meant the signing-on of new crews and the commissioning of a sizeable fleet of new ships sailing under national flags. But the vital point to notice is that all were still sailing ships; all still depended upon the same winds; very much the same charts were to be found in all of them; and it mattered less than might have been expected whether the compass pointed the helmsmen to 'Holy Church' or 'Holy Scripture'.

But ever more obviously as these vessels breasted the waters of the eighteenth and nineteenth centuries, they found themselves caught in the tides and cross-currents of the new knowledge, the questioning of all charts and compasses alike—indeed, of the worthwhileness of any voyage at all aboard such antiquated craft, amidst so many hazards and uncertainties. It is this situation, in its most acute form, with which we are now, in the second half of the twentieth century, concerned. But our response to it will be very greatly affected by how we interpret it. How far is it a case, as it was a century ago, of a revolutionary challenge to many features of the Christian faith, and a call to a vastly enlarged conception of its implications, forced home upon us by the indubitable facts of history and of physical, biological and social science? Or, on the other hand, how far is it a case, as it was at the time of the 'old' Reformation, of the breaking out of long pent up opposition to the claims of the ecclesiastical institution and the recovery of certain basic Christian insights which had by it been for long increasingly obscured? Or yet again, how far is it, as it was in the third and fourth centuries, a response to powerful pressures upon the Christian faith to surrender its distinctive affirmations and valuations in order to accommodate itself to the alleged requirements of 'the modern mind'?

To examine some of the considerations bearing upon such questions as these will be the main concern of the next chapter. But before looking at them I want to try to bring out in a little more detail the implications of the contrast between the 'old' and the 'new' Reformations which I have so far indicated only in the broadest sense. I want to suggest that the radical differences between them can best be brought out by noticing the differences between the questions to which the two movements attempt respectively to give answers.

We may well feel that Horst Symanowski misrepresents both

movements by trying to bring the contrast within the scope of
only two questions—'How can I find a gracious God?' and
'How can I find a gracious neighbour?'[51] Yet the fact remains
that the two movements are concerned with two distinct
orders of questions. The leaders of the Reformation of the
sixteenth century were united in an unshakeable confidence in
the reality of God, of his self-revelation in history and above
all in Jesus; they were unanimous in believing that there is a
gospel to be proclaimed; they accepted the reality of the church
charged with the responsibility of proclaiming and witnessing
to this gospel and of shepherding all those who are brought
into the obedience of faith. Furthermore, they all believed that
a man's eternal destiny, whether of bliss or of torment,
depended upon his response in this life to the message of
salvation proclaimed to him.

The questions which divided the Reformers collectively from
the Roman church and also often divided them from one
another were such questions as these. How does God reveal
himself to men? Is it mainly through the divinely ordained and
supernatural medium of the church as an institution? Or
through the infallible Bible and the preached word? Or in the
mystic quest of the enlightened soul? How is God to be wor-
shipped? By means of cultic practices which can be shown to be
continuous with those of the Old and New Testaments? Or is
there a rightful place for development of forms and orders
whose origins cannot thus be traced to Biblical precedents?
What is the true form of the church? Is it composed of all who,
under the pressure of custom and of the secular authority are
brought into it by baptism in infancy? Or is it composed only
of those who have made a conscious and responsible profession

[51] Symanowski (Horst) *The Christian Witness in an Industrial Society*.
Philadelphia: Westminster Press, 1964. cf. Robinson (John) *The New
Reformation?* London: SCM, 1965, pp. 32-3.

of faith and a resolve of amendment of life? What are the grounds and limits of its authority? Is there any place in it for imposition of beliefs and the coercion of physical sanctions? How is its authority related to that of the magistrate?

It would be true, I believe, to suggest that the different churches which grew out of the Reformation movement of the sixteenth century were shaped by the different answers which came to be given to such questions as these. But between then and now lies the 'great divide', or the 'great transition', and in particular the philosophical and theological transformations which have occurred since the eighteenth century. If, scientifically speaking, it was a mistake to have been born before Darwin, it could equally well be said that, philosophically speaking, it was a mistake to have been born before Kant. Of the revolution in thought for which he had so large a responsibility it has been said that it 'separates from their forbears men who have lived since Kant by a greater interval than that which divided Kant from Plato'.[52] For what Kant did was to show that the human mind is so constituted that rational discourse can give certainty only in relation to the finite and the phenomenal. In this way he placed an inescapable question mark against all the confident assertions and reasonings concerning God and divine things, whether by a Calvin, a Grotius, a Bellarmine or a Barclay. As a consequence, the matters concerning which the sixteenth-century Reformers were so sure are among the very matters about which we who live in the period of the new Reformation are likely to be least sure. We are asking whether the word 'God' can be known to stand for any reality that can 'reveal' anything at all. We are uncertain as to whether there is a 'gospel' which is the same for all men everywhere, and even if there were we are pretty sure that a

[52] Caldwell-Moore (E.) *Christian Thought since Kant.* London: Duckworth, 1912, p. 5.

man's eternal destiny is not determined irrevocably by his response to it in this life. We are far from sure whether the church, in any form recognisably related to any of its traditional patterns has any longer relevance to contemporary life. We press the question whether worship in any sense distinguishable from meditation or the cultivation of certain attitudes of mind or states of consciousness any longer makes sense to modern people. We raise the question, even, whether any religious assertions of any kind can be regarded as 'true' or as 'making sense' on account of the inherent limitations of language.

The fact seems to be that the kinds of answers which men today give to such questions as these bear little relation to the traditional answers given hitherto to the Reformers' questions by the churches to which they belong. A modern Christian's answers to today's radical questions depend far less upon whether he is an Anglican, a Baptist or a Quaker than they do upon whether he is above or below the age of thirty, whether he has received a university education, whether his training is in the physical sciences and technology or in the arts or the social sciences.

One way of putting this might be to say that divisions between the churches of the old Reformation are, so to speak, vertical divisions, constituted by their distinctively different answers to the kinds of question raised in the sixteenth and seventeenth centuries. But the types of answer given by contemporary Christians to the questions being raised by the new Reformation cut right across these traditional denominational answers; they follow lines of cleavage which are, so to speak, horizontal. They divide between those who, for example, can use 'God-language' and those who cannot; between those for whom worship is essentially soliloquy and those for whom it is in some sense a hearing and a dialogue; between those for

33

whom salvation means primarily security in the world to come and those for whom it means primarily the abandonment of all security save that involved in becoming servants of the divine purpose in and for this world. Of course, not all contemporary Christians will find themselves in the same camp with the same companions in relation to all such questions. But the implications of this analysis are far-reaching, and the next two chapters will seek to draw out some of the most important of them.

III

THE NEW REFORMATION—WHAT HAVE FRIENDS TO SAY?

In the previous chapters, I have tried to set out, with the minimum of evaluation, some features of four main emphases of the new Reformation movement, and to offer some considerations which may help to explain why these emphases are being made at this particular time. In the present chapter I propose to offer some comments of an evaluative kind concerning these same four emphases. As has been recognised more than once already, the new Reformation is a term which covers much that is of genuine and permanent significance and also some things that may well be of only quite transient importance, things that should be recognised as being even mistaken or unjustified. In making these comments I want, in the first place, to try to reflect the views of those who, so far as I can judge, have given the most informed and sustained thought to these matters and whose opinions should therefore be listened to with respect. Then I shall venture to make a few comments, in each of the four areas, from a quite frankly Quaker point of view, drawing attention to some things with which Friends may feel generally able to unite and other things about which they may justifiably feel 'stops in the mind'.

But before going further, I should, perhaps, make a comment on the influence upon all these areas of discussion of what is usually called the linguistic philosophy or logical empiricism.

In so far as the linguistic philosophy is a warning against an over-valuing of the ability of words to express and convey spiritual realities, and of the ability of rational argumentation to establish religious truths, it is exerting an influence with which most Friends will feel a good measure of unity. Its emphasis upon the need constantly to question the meaning of religious assertions and to test them against the facts of our experience is also congenial to Friends. But in so far as, in the hands of some of its exponents it has been an instrument for denying the validity of all religious experience, or of insisting that religious assertions must be tested by the same criteria as apply to sense experience and the methods of the physical sciences, Friends will not be alone in questioning whether it has not exceeded its measure.

The Radical Theology

In the previous chapters I tried to show that the radical theology is part of a comprehensive and variegated reaction to an unprecedentedly wide and rapid transformation in human knowledge and power. This transformation is very recent; we are all of us caught up in its effects, and all the signs point towards its being still only in its early stages.

In this unstable situation, is there anything that can usefully be said in a few paragraphs about what has come to be called 'the debate about God'? I believe there are at least three things. First of all, we need to be clear about what kind of issue we are raising when we ask such questions as 'Can we any longer believe in God?' We are not simply raising a question about the possibility, in the light of modern knowledge of the universe, of there being somewhere in it a Being possessing in a supreme degree certain attributes of power, wisdom, immortality and the like. Even if the existence of such a Being could be 'proved'—which it cannot be—this would not be the God of Christian faith. The question we are really raising is a much more important one. In fact, the meaningfulness of all other questions and answers will turn upon our answer to it. We are raising the question whether, when all is said and done, words such as 'meaning' and 'value' point to something 'really real'; or whether they merely register our personal preferences, determined as these may be in the last resort by heredity, social pressures or the secretions of our glands. This, I believe, is the central question at issue.

Hitherto, the answers to this question have been based to a large extent upon the deliverances of allegedly divinely inspired persons, the authority of sacred writings and institutions or else upon the constructions of comprehensive metaphysical world-views. Today, however, all these types of answer are deeply suspect by many people. Does this mean that there is no evidence upon which an answer to this central question can be based? I believe not. On the contrary, I believe that precisely at this time we are being challenged by aspects of our experience which, if we rightly discern their implications, can restore to us in a relevant contemporary form a sense of the reality of God.

For example, the very sciences which, in the opinion of many, have put a final question mark against the existence of God, have demonstrated that the world of our experience is not a 'monotonous succession of disconnected sights and sounds'. Our relations with one another, and our experience of beauty in artistic creation open our eyes to recognise 'structures of moral and aesthetic values'. But if we recognise that this is so, can we reasonably evade the larger question which these facts suggest? The 'debate about God' is a debate about whether our world is 'merely an island in a sea of meaninglessness', about whether we do not, in our experience, when it is deeply enough understood, 'touch something that is universal, something that gives unifying meaning to the totality of our existence.'[53]

[53] Bennett (John C.) in *Radical Theology: Phase Two: essays in a continuing discussion*, ed. C. W. Christian and G. R. Wittig. Philadelphia: Lippincott, 1967, p. 141 ff.

Again, it is precisely in these days, when we are rightly being warned against the dangers both of the cultivation of pious interior attitudes and also of attempting to construct comprehensive philosophical systems, that we are rediscovering the fact that there is laid upon us a sense of obligation to certain courses of action which is absolute. Does not this strongly suggest that, through our recognition of moral obligation, we are aware of a demand which does not originate with us, but which we come to recognise as 'there'? In this respect, I believe it is not altogether wide of the mark to claim that what is being rediscovered in the civil rights movements, the opposition to apartheid, the anti-war protests, as well as in schemes of voluntary aid in developing countries, is something very close to the insight of the Hebrew prophets that to do justly, to show compassion for the oppressed, the fatherless and the widow is in fact to 'know God'.[54] In other words, we might express the point I am wanting to make by saying that all these activities finally make sense *only if* there is, in the structure of Being itself, the concern for justice, integrity, truth and compassion. Something like this is, I believe, the substance of belief in the reality of God, and it is a stronger argument than any brought against belief in the reality of God by those who understand the radical theology as involving a literal atheism.

The second thing that needs to be said about the radical theology relates to that feature of it which has been somewhat unkindly yet not altogether inaccurately expressed in the phrase 'God is dead; long live Jesus'. The attempt to make the human Jesus and his attitudes fill the whole gap left by the 'death' of God cannot succeed. In the first place, it assumes far too uncritically that the historical evidence concerning the human character and attitudes of Jesus is more complete and unequivocal than it is. It also seriously underestimates the

[54] *Jeremiah*, xxii, 15-16 and *Micah*, vi, 8.

extent to which the facts that we do possess concerning Jesus were preserved precisely because, for those who remembered and transmitted them, the significance of Jesus was that he pointed men to God, his Father, and taught men to understand his own life in relation to the will and purpose of God which found expression through him. But, most important of all, it is surely impossible to doubt that the source of his living 'for others', of his 'contagious freedom', is none other than his profound awareness of his relation to 'the Father'. It has been well said that 'Jesus without Jesus' heavenly Father simply is not Jesus'.[55]

A third point which can, I believe, be legitimately made concerns the serious extent to which, in much of the radical theology, the conception of God which is rejected is not the distinctively Christian one at all. Sometimes it is almost indistinguishable from a frankly deistic one, or even one which is closer to the Islamic than to the Christian understanding. The God who is a 'working hypothesis', who is the 'explanation' of what would otherwise be inexplicable, the 'God-of-the-gaps', the *deus ex machina*—all these are no doubt legitimate targets for destructive criticism. But at what point does such criticism damage the classical Christian doctrine of God? According to this, there is in God a richness or complexity of being such that at one and the same time he is the source and ground from which all being is derived, manifests his character and purpose in nature and in history and, mysteriously working within his creation, enables it to respond to his purpose in ways which respect and preserve its genuine contingency and freedom. Here, surely, although necessarily expressed in the merest 'shorthand', is a conception of God which offers clues to some of our deepest intuitions and maturest reflections, and lies far

---

[55] Baelz (P. R.) Is God Real? *Faith, Fact and Fantasy*, ed. C. F. D. Moule. London: Collins (Fontana), 1964, p. 60.

beyond the range of sniping from merely positivistic, naturalistic and linguistic premisses.

The more I read and reflect upon the whole radical theology controversy, the more I am disposed to agree with the view of it expressed in the concluding paragraph of David Jenkins' admirable *Guide to the Debate About God*. 'I would argue that what the "debate about God" particularly shows us is not that God cannot be believed in, but that in much at any rate of Western Christian theism He has as a matter of fact not been believed in. We have practised religious idolatry rather than the obedient and expectant worship of the living God.'[56] David Jenkins makes a no less telling point when he observes, earlier in the same book, that 'a God in whom any one found it easy to believe would be a particularly futile idol'.[57] It has never been the claim of a well founded Christian apologetic that it can make the doctrine of God self-evidently and compellingly clear. The hiddenness or reticence of God has always been an integral part of the Hebrew, Biblical, Christian understanding of God. The Old Testament refusal of material images of God is surely a parable and a warning. It contains, indeed, passages which tell of God speaking to Moses face to face, as a man speaks with his friend;[58] but it also contains passages which recognise that no man can see God's face and live.[59] Likewise, Job, to whom at the end of his travail a vision of the majesty of God is finally granted, cries out in a passion of self-abnegation: 'I abhor myself and repent in dust and ashes.'[60] For if God is indeed the Being in whom we live and move and have our being, his reality can never be 'proved' or 'disproved' by the methods appropriate to the investigation of particular

[56] Jenkins (David) *Guide to the Debate About God*. London: Lutterworth, 1966, p. 109.
[57] *Ibid.*, p. 81.
[58] *Exodus*, xxxiii, 11.
[59] *Exodus*, xxxiii, 20, cf. *Genesis*, xxxii, 30.
[60] *Job*, xlii, 6.

finite beings. Nor is his reality to be known by the detached, critical intellect. He is to be known only when what is at stake is nothing less than the significance of our whole existence in face of all that threatens to overwhelm it. And, so great is the mystery of his Being that it is of his mercy that we are covered by the shadow of his hand when he is nearest to us.[61]

If all this had been more generally understood, I believe it would have been seen to be a mistake to imagine that the reality of God must be rejected in the interest of man's mature acceptance of responsible existence. The wise words of a Roman Catholic layman[62] express a profound truth. 'The feelings of belief we cherish, the images and habitual attitudes which occupy us when we pray or speak of him, are not God . . . Conventional language about God is dead, and some conventional religious institutions are useless where they are not harmful. But those who have daily eaten the bread of naked faith have not drawn their sustenance from "the religious age". Correspondingly, they are not frightened by its passing.' At their best, surely, Quakers have always known this. They have always known that a belief in God and a denial of God can, both alike, rest on 'notional' grounds. We need, perhaps, to paraphrase George Fox's famous words to read: 'Bultmann says this, and Tillich and Altizer and Hamilton say this—but what canst thou say?' And we also need to remind ourselves that what we say *about* God is far less important than what we say *in response to* God. What we say in response to him is being said in all the innumerable circumstances of daily living, and only when these circumstances are seen thus as the symbols both of God's presence and of our response are they redeemed from triviality.

[61] *Exodus*, xxxiii, 22.
[62] Novak (Michael) in *Radical Theology: Phase Two: essays in a continuing discussion*, ed. C. W. Christian and G. R. Wittig. Philadelphia: Lippincott, 1967, p. 157 ff.

41

An illuminating essay by David Jenkins entitled 'Whither the Doctrine of God Now?'[63] speaks of the determination of 'post-Copernican Man' to 'put everything to the test of experience and experiment and to proceed inductively from the knowledge he has to the building up of further knowledge'. If this correctly describes the attitude characteristic of ourselves and of most of our contemporaries, and I believe it does, it may indicate to us as Friends what our particular task in relation to the radical theology may be. For, traditionally and characteristically, Friends have never felt the need to propose a new doctrine of God. Nor have they felt the foundations of their lives threatened by 'new theologies'. They have been sure that the reality of God lies deeper, and is made known not to those who possess the fullest and clearest ideas of God but to those who, with humility, patience and integrity seek to respond to his witness in themselves and to raise up that witness in others. Friends ought to be ready, therefore, to recognise the truth of Jenkins' claim that 'no doctrine of God can go forward unless it is clearly related to a spiritual discipline and discipleship which is experiential and experimental in relation both to the Tradition and to the current situation'. Such discipline and discipleship, he continues, 'must emerge from and be backed up by a Christian community which is plainly living experimentally and openly'. Could the Society of Friends play a more significant part in the promotion of the 'new Reformation' than by seeking above all to be precisely such a community?

Secularity

If, in the popular mind, the radical theology has come to be understood as a rejection of God, then the current concern with secularity and 'religionlessness' and man's 'coming of age' may

[63] Jenkins (David) Whither the Doctrine of God Now? *The London Quarterly and Holborn Review*, July 1964.

be said to be understood as an acceptance of the world. Neither is an accurate or just estimate; but together they will serve to indicate the central issue about which a few comments must now be made. Is it true that only a death-of-God theology is able to inspire and give scope for a truly mature and responsible dealing with the contemporary world? Must God 'die' to make room for the 'maturity' of modern man? Can the essence of Christian faith and life be completely expressed through social, political and economic involvement?

We should begin by reminding ourselves that the radical theology is a changing and developing thing, and that there is already evidence of a certain trend or tendency in its development. This fact is brought out very clearly by the editors of the first three volumes of *New Theology*.[64] After selecting what they regard as the most significant contributions during the present decade to more than two hundred theological journals, they draw attention to a trend away from 'centrifugality and apparent anarchy' in much theological discussion, and towards 'a kind of centripetal direction, a hunger for order, a courage to make affirmations in the context of Christian tradition, a hesitant but visible first step towards new construction'. They detect a renewed interest in 'talk about God', and concern for 'some sense of program for church life in the "secular city" '. In their opinion, these trends are not unconnected with the fact that, by many serious students, much of the radical theology in its earlier phases has been seen to be 'short-range, sterile, devoid of content'. They note, too, that 'secular intellectuals and other non-churched compatriots have not been visibly more drawn to the "secular" theology than to its more burdened and apparently arcane antecedents in orthodoxy and neo-orthodoxy'. They conclude: 'In any case,

[64] Marty (Martin E.) and Peerman (Dean G.) eds. *New Theology*, Vols. I, II & III. London: Collier-Macmillan, 1965-7.

4

countertrends are visible, reaction is setting in, options are present, issues are joined, a debate is in progress. The signs of a new order—though not of a new conservatism or repressivism—impress us as we read these journals' pages.'

This, then, is the context in which we need to look at the issues with which this section deals. It suggests at once, surely, that there is no need to accept hastily the sharp alternatives in which they have often been expressed. We are not shut up to a stark choice between an interest in and responsible concern for the world of time and space and a recognition of the reality and claims of a world which lies beyond these categories. Nor do we have to regard time spent in worship and prayer as so much time lost or wasted which should have been devoted to demonstrating, organising political and social movements or becoming involved in various forms of humanitarian service.

To say this is not to imply that the current concern with secularity, religionless Christianity and modern man's coming of age are to be dismissed, or that they have not an important point to make. The Christian churches have unquestionably been guilty, over long periods of their history, of showing sinfully small concern for the material and physical conditions of men's lives, and of justifying this lack of concern by calling in the other world, not to redress the balance of this one, but rather to justify or divert attention from its manifest imbalance. For vast numbers of modern people, traditional forms of religion have almost no meaning or relevance. Whatever faith they may be said to exhibit is faith in the power of science, technology and planning either to provide whatever good things are possible in the only life man has, or else to do what is possible to compensate for or provide distractions from its inevitable and progressive frustrations.

As I have already mentioned in a preceding chapter, the related themes of secularity, religionlessness and maturity have been given enthusiastic and widely influential expression in Harvey Cox's *The Secular City*. In that book the unprecedented, accelerating and inexorable growth of 'technopolis' is celebrated rather than described. It is seen as the contemporary form assumed by the divine purpose for man. Its cultural, political, social and economic structures are held to provide the sufficient framework for Christian living. Its attitudes and values and opportunities are the data in relation to which Christians are to give expression to the attitudes exemplified by Jesus.

What is to be said in response to all this? In the first place, it seems to me to be entirely right that Christians should be encouraged to look positively on the tremendous changes and developments among which our lives are set, discerning as far as possible the opportunities which they provide for existence in concerned and responsible community. But, on the other hand, it may well be that Cox and others seriously underestimate the negative, destructive and alienating forces which are present in urban mass society. Their presence is certainly very clear to some of the most sensitive and perceptive novelists, poets and playwrights of our time, not to mention such sociologists as Jacques Ellul.[65]

Again, we may well agree that a church which is not at as many points as possible seriously engaged with the problems, challenges and opportunities presented by the contemporary world is not fulfilling its role as part of the one church. But this is not to say that the whole being of a church is exhausted in such engagement and involvement. There must still, surely, be a place for a church to be concerned with the nurture, teaching, care and discipline of a committed membership, equipping them through worship and supporting them by fellowship in a

[65] Ellul (Jacques) *Technological Society*. New York: Knopf, 1965, *passim*.

common life for their service in the world. In other words, commitment to the church's task in the world commits one to a recognition of the continuing and increasing importance of the church as a religious community, with whatever traditional and institutional features are necessary for its continuity and growth. A 'religionless' Christianity which implies the abolition or withering away of the church is as unrealistic and has as little to commend it as an ecclesiastical Christianity which sees the world as important only as a source of recruitment and support for the church. Furthermore, it is not clear by what logic Harvey Cox, and those who think like him, appear to hold that the morally ambiguous structures of the churches considered as institutions prevent their being of service to the divine purpose which, nevertheless, is apparently well able to operate through the no less morally ambiguous institutional structures of 'technopolis'.

Another point at which Cox and van Leeuwen (see p. 16 above) are open to criticism is their claim that secularisation as expressed in the world-embracing dynamism of western civilisation is to be understood as the contemporary form of the Biblical kingdom of God. This is surely going too far. It may indeed be true that the Hebrew-Biblical-Christian world view did in fact do much to prepare the soil in which scientific enquiry flourished and, in time, produced technological and urban civilisation. But it must be recognised that the scientific attitude of mind owes at least as much to Greek as to Biblical presuppositions. And it is arguable that western civilisation has forfeited any right it might have had to be regarded as the contemporary expression of the kingdom by its excesses and insensitivities, and by its indiscriminate and overwhelming destructiveness of all that has stood in its way.

A further reflection may give us cause to question some of the more thorough-going exponents of secularity and religionlessness. Much of their argument appears to rest upon certain assumptions concerning 'modern man', and what he is capable or incapable of taking seriously and believing. But an answer to the question 'Who is this modern man whose outlook you take to be so decisive?' is far to seek in their writings. They appear to ignore the fact that many people with an unquestionable right to be considered fully modern, do in reality, and after careful examination, accept and hold these 'impossible' beliefs because they know in their own experience the reality which these beliefs, as symbols, seek to express and interpret. It is far from obvious, also, why it should be assumed that man come of age is man grown beyond the need or the possibility of religion. If it is reasonable to regard modern man—i.e. urbanised and industrialised man—as mature, it is reasonable to think that what he needs and seeks is maturity of religious experience and belief, not their abandonment.

The point that has to be made is that any insight into and concern for the human condition which has any claim to be called Christian is an insight and a concern deriving from certain beliefs. These beliefs are expressed in such doctrines as those of the creation and the Incarnation, of sin and grace. If these beliefs point to truth, if they open our eyes to see the way things actually are, then they also relate us to sources of compassion and endurance which would not be available but for these beliefs. And it has yet to be shown that any other sources exist which can inspire and sustain the attitudes which the world, for its healing, so desperately needs.

Paul Tillich pointed us in the right direction when he spoke of the need to go beyond both 'heteronomy' and 'autonomy', beyond both the acceptance (as by many merely conventionally religious people) of a purely external ultimate authority, and the rejection (as by the thoroughgoing secularist) of any ultimate reality to which we are responsible. Beyond both these positions lies what Tillich called 'theonomy', the recognition that our own reality as particular beings derives from, is sustained by and finds its goal and fulfilment in that fount and fullness of being to which the religious man points by the word God.

At the present time, more than one philosophical and linguistic pattern is available to us for the expression of such a position. We may emphasise the concepts of process and evolution; or we may make central an exploration of the meaning of human existence in its frailty and finiteness; or we may concentrate upon the elucidation of the behaviour and meaning of religious language. All three approaches are of value; none needs to exclude what is valid in the others; each will speak to the condition of some people more than others; together they give us all the scope that a Christian emphasis upon the significance of secularity requires. I am inclined to think that these words of Bonhoeffer[66] express what needs to be said in this connection: 'In Christ we are offered the possibility of partaking in the reality of God and in the reality of the world, but not in the one without the other. The reality of God discloses itself only by setting me entirely in the reality of the world, and when I encounter the reality of the world it is always already sustained, accepted and reconciled in the reality of God.'

The general 'thrust' of much contemporary secular or religionless Christianity is one with which many Friends will feel a good deal of sympathy. It is no new thing, in our corporate experience, to stress the need to express our faith in concrete action in the secular world, to ignore or deny any ultimate distinction between the sacred and the secular. We have never hesitated to point to the dangers inherent in much merely traditional or conventional religion, and its impotence

[66] Bonhoeffer (D.) *Ethics*. London: SCM, 1955, p. 61.

to effect a moral transformation in life. But such weight as these criticisms had was due to our own no less sustained witness to the reality of God, to the possibility of cultivating a sensitive awareness of his presence and an obedient readiness to obey his requirements. In other words, our 'secularity' has been the fruit of our beliefs, and these have been discerned and validated in our corporate experience. May it not be that, in describing the church's crucial task today, Karl Rahner, perhaps one of the greatest living Roman Catholic thinkers, is describing exactly the task to which we need to devote ourselves as a religious society? It is the task of so bearing faithful witness to 'the redeeming and fulfilling presence of that ineffable mystery whom we call God that the men of the age of technology, who have already made so many advances toward control of their world and destiny, can experience the power of this unspeakable mystery in their lives'.[67] Is this not another way of saying that we are to 'answer that of God in every man'?

'New Morality' or 'Situational ethics'

In much the same way as the radical theology has crystallised, in the minds of many people, into the single issue of whether or not, or in what sense, God is 'dead', and the question of secularity has resolved itself into the question whether or not 'the world' can and should provide not only the setting but also the norms and motivations of the Christian's daily life, so the ethical question has tended to become polarised into a debate between a 'legalistic' and a 'situational' approach.

This way of posing the ethical question has certainly had some positive effects. It has rightly emphasised the supremacy of personal values and of the importance of remedial and

[67] Rahner (Karl) *The Church After the Council*. New York: Herder, 1966, p. 26.

reconciliatory aims. It has provided a salutary reminder of the enormous complexity and variety of the situations in which we have to try to make responsible ethical decisions. It rightly warns against the sterility of a loveless legalism, and raises an altogether justified warning against the danger of treating even the Sermon on the Mount as a new law.

Yet there is, I think, a growing recognition that this way of posing the question, for all its emphasis on 'the situation', fails to take account of some very important aspects of the general situation with which ethics as a whole deals. As Professor H. E. W. Turner said of John Robinson's treatment of 'The New Morality' in *Honest to God*, it gives 'vigorous expression to something like half the truth'.[68]

The way in which this oversimplification of the ethical question has tended to divert the discussion into a dead end is admirably analysed by Professor James M. Gustafson in a paper entitled 'Context versus Principles; a misplaced Debate in Christian Ethics'.[69] After illustrating the various senses in which both 'context' or 'situation' and also 'principles' are understood and used by different writers, Gustafson concludes that the debate in these terms has become 'both academically unjust and increasingly morally fruitless'. It is clear, he argues, that 'contextualists find some moral principles or generalizations that give guidance to existential decisions, and that the defenders of principles find some ways to proceed from generalizations to particular situations'. He then goes on to show that any fruitful discussions of Christian ethics must make reference to four 'base-points'. These are (a) 'as accurate and perceptive social or situational analysis as possible'; (b) funda-

[68] Turner (H. E. W.) in *The Honest to God Debate*, ed. D. L. Edwards. London: SCM, 1963, p. 153.
[69] *Harvard Theological Review*, April, 1965, reprinted in *New Theology*, ed. M. E. Marty and D. G. Pearman, vol. 3. London: Collier-Macmillan, 1967, pp. 69-103.

mental theological affirmations; (c) moral principles; (d) 'the nature of the Christian's life in Christ'. He proceeds to argue convincingly that, whichever of these base-points a given ethicist may take as his point of departure, he will be bound to bring the other three into his purview if his work is to be both realistic and Christian.

A similar line of criticism is advanced by Professor Paul Ramsey in his *Deeds and Rules in Christian Ethics*. Following Professor W. K. Frankena, he recognises that Christian ethics bases itself upon the concept of *agape* rather than upon that of moral duty or upon some principle of utility. But to recognise that 'agapism' is the distinctive quality of any ethic entitled to be called Christian does not mean that the upholder of rules or principles is necessarily to be regarded as having abandoned *agape* as the basis of Christian ethics. There is an 'act-agapism' and there is a 'rule-agapism'. 'Theologians today', says Ramsey, 'are simply deceiving themselves and playing tricks with their readers when they pit the freedom and ultimacy of *agape* . . . against rules, without asking whether *agape* can and may or must work through rules and embody itself in certain principles which are regulative or the guidance of practice.'[70] On the basis of this recognition that *agape* can and should express itself both in acts and rules, Ramsey makes a searching examination of the ethical argumentation of the pamphlet *Towards a Quaker View of Sex*.[71] He finds that, although the arguments of the pamphlet point towards the recognition that there are, indeed, 'rules of action embodying Christian responsibility in sexual behaviour', its authors 'flinched and drew back' from this conclusion, and put forward

[70] Ramsey (Paul) *Deeds and Rules in Christian Ethics*. Scottish Journal of Theology. Occasional Papers No. 11. Edinburgh: Oliver & Boyd, 1965, p. 4.
[71] Heron (A.) ed. *Towards a Quaker View of Sex*. Revised edition. London: Friends Home Service Committee, 1964.

instead a doctrine of 'act-agapism', thus vitiating the force of what is otherwise recognised to be a serious and profound attempt to deal with its theme.

The comments I have so far made have been made from an analytical standpoint, and have aimed at breaking down the sharp antithesis which has come to be accepted between love and law, the 'situation' and the rule or principle. But comments which attempt to place the contemporary ethical debate in an historical perspective may also be relevant. A little earlier in this discussion I referred to the four base-points of any worthwhile treatment of Christian ethics. The one of these which has received least attention in the current debate is the fourth, 'the nature of the Christian's life in Christ'. It has been too readily assumed, I think, that the discernment of the nature of love and of the concrete action which love may require in any given situation, as well as the resources upon which that love can draw if it is to persist, are relatively independent of what is believed. But this, surely, is not the case. It is, I believe, a fact of history that an altogether new dimension of the meaning of love began to permeate the Roman world in the first century of this era; and it permeated it because and in so far as a community of men and women believed certain things to be true, learned the discipline of love in a closely-knit corporate life, and knew themselves committed to extend that love to those who hitherto had never experienced it. As Professor T. E. Jessop has said of the new ethical possibilities which were then explored and demonstrated, 'the new morality . . . was impossible apart from the new religion'.[72] If this was true, as I believe it was, in Roman society of the first century, can we expect an equally creative contemporary morality long to survive the passing of the Christian beliefs and community experience in which it was born and nourished?

[72] Jessop (T. E.) *The Christian Morality*. London: Epworth, 1960, p. 55.

Another relevant historical consideration concerns the transformation which progressively changed the Christian moral outlook from the fourth century onward. With the coming into being of what has been called the Constantinian synthesis, by which the secular authority conferred privilege, protection and prestige upon the church and, in return, received from the church blessing and support, citizenship and membership of the church became practically coterminous. This came to mean that the church no longer expected of its whole membership the heroic ethical standards of an earlier period. It also meant that the church came to see its discharge of its moral obligations in political terms rather than in terms of radical internal discipline. The church called upon the secular authority to deal by legislation with moral evils which it showed itself unable to deal with effectively by means of its own sacramental and penitential system. Or else it simply accepted these evils as inevitable, and limited itself to minimising some of their more obvious effects or symptoms.

From the point of view of this discussion, the important matter to emphasise is that the Constantinian synthesis has now come to an end, in Catholic and Protestant forms alike. No longer is it acceptable anywhere that the church should have the authority to regulate or influence moral conduct by means of prescriptive codes and legal sanctions. But the alternative to this is not for the churches to refrain from speaking clearly and courageously on ethical issues. Neither should they accept the assumption that the secular Christian has access to no other resources of insight, motivation and perseverance than are available to the secular non-Christian. Rather, the vacuum left in the sphere of Christian ethics by the collapse of the Constantinian, medieval and main-line Protestant ethical assumptions needs to be filled by the recovery of the characteristically Christian ethical possibilities. It has been well said that

' "new morality" is a highly secondary need to "new disciple-ship". And new discipleship is going to emerge when we hold with equal openness and tenacity both to the modern secular world and to the contemporary Christ.'[73] It may well be that the churches' ethical pronouncements will be taken with much greater seriousness by the secular world when they are seen to be addressed primarily to the committed membership of the churches, and are also seen to be actually obeyed by that membership. As Martin Buber once remarked, the churches have too often summoned nations and peoples to accept risks which the churches themselves have not demonstrated their own willingness to run.[74]

It is at this point, I think, that a more specifically Quaker comment may be in order, and it is a comment which will amplify a little the relation between 'new morality' and 'new discipleship'. The feature of Quakerism which has always attracted the most positive notice has been its ethical sensitivity and creativeness. Friends have been led to feel the ethical challenge and obligation which have long been contained in familiar evils but obscured by conventional acceptance of them. They have responded, not by the imposition of any legalistic ethical code, but by opening themselves to the true inwardness of each actual situation. This is not a mere extem-porism, a reliance upon unmediated individualistic inspiration. But what they have seen in any given situation has been determined by their conviction that, in every situation, there is a hidden presence of God to be discerned and answered, that the true sufferer under every injustice, cruelty and oppression is the Christ. And Friends have been able thus to interpret every situation for two reasons. First, they shared a common

[73] Vincent (J. J.) *Here I Stand; the Faith of a Radical*. London: Epworth, 1967, p. 45.
[74] Gollwitzer (H.) quotes this of Martin Buber in *Therefore Choose Life*, ed. A. H. Silver. London: Barmerlea, 1967.

framework of belief, in which was central the conviction of God's creative and saving presence in the world. And, second, they nurtured and practised this belief and this sensitivity in a community life in which they accepted its requirements and discovered its resources before they went out to commend it to others. May it not be that, in rediscovering this experience, we may be able to make the most relevant contribution of which we are capable to the discovery and implementation of a truly new morality?

The structures and relationships of the churches

Already, in previous sections of this chapter, I have found it necessary, in the course of the discussion of the implications of the 'new theology', the 'new morality' and the Christian concern with the secular, to refer several times to the subject of the church. It is now necessary for us to try to gain a vantage point from which the broad outlines of the contemporary concern with the church, its nature, structures and relationships, can be viewed, and to offer a few considerations which may help us to take our bearings on it. Here, if anywhere, the need is for large maps.

It seems to me that there are three features which are characteristic of this current interest in the church. The first is derived from the recognition on the part of modern Biblical and theological study of the central importance, in both Hebrew and Christian traditions, of the concept of 'the people of God'. It would not, I think, be too much to say that the whole Bible is now seen to be primarily concerned, not with tracing the development of progressively loftier religious ideas, nor with reflecting the inner spiritual experiences of outstandingly pious individuals, but rather with the gathering and training of a concrete community of men and women to bear a

55

corporate witness to the character of God and to become the agents of his purpose of reconciliation in the world.

This means that it is no longer possible to view the church simply as an adjunct to the gospel; it is an integral part of it. The gospel, the good news of supreme importance, is nothing less than the proclamation and demonstration that there is at work in the world of historical existence a divine purpose to gather, harmonise, unify and free from frustration the scattered and discordant purposes of men. This purpose works in and through the society in which men are to find the vision of the true end of life, an experience of that end even in the midst of life, and the motivation and power for the bringing into relation to that end ever wider and more comprehensive areas of existence.

To recognise something like this to be the true nature and purpose of the church is, inevitably, to recognise also the tragic and bitter contrast between such a vision and the actual historical features and conditions of the churches: and this brings before us the second feature to which I want to invite attention. There is now a general recognition that we must draw a clear distinction between this vision of the essence of the church and the limited, imperfect and often even sordid historical and institutional forms in which that vision has been and is embodied—and obscured. This means that there is now a readiness on the part of adherents of practically all the various churches to recognise how much their various institutional forms have been and are influenced by the contingency and transitoriness of history. There is therefore much less readiness than in the past to claim permanent validity and divine sanction for any given form, order or structure. There is also now, as never before, a recognition that we cannot claim that the actual course taken by the main streams of the church's life is the course that was divinely intended. This means that there is a growing recognition that the main traditions of the church may indeed have taken wrong turnings in the past, that some of the heretical groups may well have had valid points to make. This means, further, that, at the present time, the path of wisdom for all of us is to open ourselves in the fullest possible manner to the requirements of today and to appropriate and interpret so much of our particular traditions as may still enable us to give appropriate expression to the vision of 'a great people to be gathered'.

This greater readiness to be discriminating in our attitude to the history of the church in general and to our own traditions in particular, leads me to notice a third important feature of the current preoccupation with the church. It is now generally recognised that in the course of its history, the church has tended to find expression in three main forms. These forms have been variously named. In ecumenical circles they have sometimes been described as 'altar-centred', 'pulpit-centred', and 'waiting upon the Spirit'. Lesslie Newbigin has attached to them the labels 'Catholic', 'Protestant' and 'Pentecostal'.[75] More recently, wide currency has been given to these distinctions, in the context of the new Reformation discussion, by the American theologian and sociologist Gibson Winter, who employs the terms 'cultic organism' or 'cultic body', 'confessional assembly' and 'prophetic fellowship' to denote them.

I can, perhaps, best bring out the main characteristics of each of these patterns of the church by quoting from Gibson Winter's treatment of them. The church as cultic body (of which the Eastern Orthodox and Roman Catholic churches are the best known examples), Winter says, 'saves man from the world of existence by incorporating him into a mystical organism'. For it, 'Proclamation . . . is the re-presentation of Christ in cultic acts, whether in the initiatory rite of baptism . . .

[75] Newbigin (Lesslie) *Household of God.* London: SCM, 1953.

or in the revitalizing event of eucharist'. Thus 'salvation and cultic participation become inseparable'.[76] The confessional assembly, 'exemplified in the main Protestant churches', by contrast 'proclaims a present relationship of for-giveness'. Its focus is upon the present moment 'as receiving and acknowledging in gratitude what has already been done once for all in the past . . . These events are not really past history, since they are present with power in the proclamation within the assembly. The church *becomes* in hearing this message'.[77] Gibson Winter brings out the contrast between these two patterns by saying that, whereas the cultic body 'assures man of a future by incorporating him into a mystical body already in possession of that future', the confessional assembly 'brings the full power of the saving event into the present moment through preaching, rooting a man in a trust-worthy past which no fearful future can shake'.[78]

The significant fact for our present purpose is the growing recognition that these two patterns of the church neither separately nor together cover the whole of the ground which the full vision of the church which I indicated earlier lays claim to. Individuals and groups in churches which approximate to both these patterns are feeling after another pattern of the church's role and structures, for they are recognising that, in their traditional forms, both the 'Catholic' and the 'Protestant' patterns are being felt by many of their own most seriously committed members to be less and less relevant to the prob-lems of the present time.

But there is a third pattern of the church which, throughout Christian history and particularly since the late medieval and early Reformation periods, groups of Christians have sought to

[76] Winter (Gibson) *New Creation as Metropolis.* New York: Macmillan, 1963, pp. 73-4.
[77] *Ibid.*, p. 75.
[78] *Ibid.*, pp. 76-7.

bear witness to and to embody. Whether we think of it as shaped by 'waiting upon the Spirit' or as expressing a 'Pentecostal' emphasis upon the renewing and enabling and community-forming power of the Spirit, or as constitutive of a fellowship which knows itself called to accept the suffering inseparable from a prophetic witness, it is a pattern the importance and relevance of which is now coming to be admitted more and more generally. I shall have more to say about this third pattern in the next chapter, and shall therefore at this point offer only one observation. It is, I believe, against the background that I have tried to suggest in the last few paragraphs that thé Society of Friends has the best opportunity of finding its true vocation. For as I understand it, Quakerism has an unrivalled claim to be considered as one of the most significant attempts to embody this third pattern of the church. The lessons of its successes and its failures to do so may yet be of the utmost significance to the church throughout the world.

But if I am right in suggesting that what I have sketched in this section is essentially what the contemporary ecumenical concern is all about, it is obvious that everything depends upon how these three patterns of the church's life and experience and structures are thought of in relation to each other. It is to be admitted, of course, that no single church or group of churches conforms perfectly and exactly to one and only one type. These types are abstractions, and all the actual churches express features of all three, so that their classification depends upon where they place their principal emphasis. But the really important questions which, beneath all the obvious and explicit matters of ecumenical discussion, are really being explored are these. Are these various understandings of the church mutually exclusive in principle, so that the true future of the church depends upon a victory of one over the other two? Or is each to be given relative justification in terms of a particular histori-

5

cal and cultural situation, so that all three can rightly coexist in different areas at the same time? Or, again, is each one to be seen as a particular emphasis, requiring to be set forth in relative isolation from others on account of the incomprehensible richness and many-sidedness of the truth of the divine purpose and activity, and therefore, perhaps, justified in going on side by side with the other emphases indefinitely? Or, finally, are these various emphases to be interpreted and understood in terms of the psychological and temperamental needs of different types of people, so that each type may find a pattern of church life congenial to his needs? It is, I suggest, in the finding of answers to such questions as these by the churches of the present that the church of the future will be shaped. And I even venture to believe that, both in the quality of its internal life and also in the characteristics of its external witness, even if not in its distinctive institutional forms, that church will bear a closer resemblance to what has, at its best, been most characteristic of the Society of Friends than it will to any of the main Christian traditions of the past.

IV

THE NEW REFORMATION—WHAT HAS IT TO SAY TO FRIENDS?

In the preceding chapters I have tried to describe and to appraise, so far as this is possible within very narrow limits of space, four main components of the new Reformation movement. In this chapter I want to try to suggest what may be the bearing of all this upon the present position and future course of the Society of Friends. Does it help us to see more clearly what the Society should be, and do, during the coming decades?

To frame the question in this way is, of course, already to make an assumption to which by no means all Friends will be prepared to agree. It is to assume that the Society as such should have a definable position, should deliberately steer a particular course. Against such an assumption many Friends will urge the view that the Society as such does not have any such obligation. It exists, they would claim, not to be the corporate expression of a common vision, but to be an association of open, seeking, experimental, pragmatically minded persons. Such people, it would be argued, associate themselves in the Society so that they may help one another in their search and their experimenting. On this view, if such a phrase as 'corporate expression of a common vision' be used at all, it can mean only that the members of the Society are held together by their common recognition of the paramount importance of perpetual openness to new truth. It is of the utmost importance, I believe, that we try to reach clearness on this point, for it seems to me beyond question that our attitude here will have decisive influence upon how we understand both the Society's corporate life and also its external influence. It will decisively determine our view of such matters as membership, discipline, and outreach, as well as the Society's ecumenical and inter-faith relations.

My own view, the grounds of which will appear, I hope, in what follows, is quite unequivocal. However much the Society has been—and still may be—in some respects and for some people, either a cave of Adullam[79] or a setting for unlimited idiosyncrasy, this was never its original purpose, nor has it ever been the explanation of its strength and creativeness. Men and women were drawn to and held in the fellowship of Friends, not simply because of their discontent with other forms of religious association, nor simply in order to express their own religious individualism, but because they were 'convinced of Truth'. And the truth of which they were convinced was not simply that an open and experimental attitude is the essential condition of honest religion—true though this is—but that such an attitude, if faithfully maintained, does in fact lead to a conviction of the reality of God's presence and power and to a commitment to his purpose in the world.

But, if it be granted, as I hope it will be by an increasing number of Friends, that the Society should be the corporate expression of a common vision, the corporate embodiment of a common experience, there is at present no agreement among Friends as to what that common vision and experience may be. This point is made with arresting force by Hugh Barbour in the concluding chapter of his important study *The Quakers in Puritan England*. After recognizing that they have succeeded in a remarkable manner in maintaining 'unity both in spirit and in organization', Hugh Barbour states his view that 'British Friends . . . face terrible problems of aimlessness'.[80] By 'aim-

---

[79] 1 *Samuel*, xxii, 1-2.
[80] Barbour (Hugh) *The Quakers in Puritan England*. New Haven, Conn: Yale Univ. Press, 1964, p. 252.

lessness' Hugh Barbour does not, I am sure, intend to imply that British Friends are indifferent, vacillating or lazy. Rather, he means that they are not agreed upon the aim which they ought corporately to be pursuing, and consequently are in danger either of simultaneously pursuing mutually incompatible aims or of settling for the view that the Society's only aim must be to support and encourage impartially its members in the pursuit of their individual aims without throwing the weight of the Society's corporate support behind one rather than another.

The Way Forward

In another place,[81] I have attempted to sketch the outline of some of the main alternative ways forward now being proposed in and for the Society, and I do not intend to go over this ground again here. But in that survey I did not state my own views as to the direction in which I personally believe the Society should move. This is what I now feel under some obligation to do. Before doing so, however, I want to draw attention to one consideration which bears on any attempt to formulate a serious opinion on this matter. It seems to me clear that the opinion one forms will be shaped to a large extent by the starting point from which one approaches it and the relative weight one gives to three aspects of this question. One may start from a careful analysis of the teaching of the early Quaker leaders, and then treat the resulting pattern as normative, judging all subsequent changes according to whether they tend to maintain or depart from that pattern. Or one may use the subsequent history of Quakerism as the basis upon which to develop a critique of the original vision, regarding that vision not as a datum, a 'faith once for all delivered', but as an

[81] Creasey (M. A.) A Frame of Reference for Friends. *Quaker Religious Thought*, no. 2, autumn 1966.

amalgam of permanently important insights and historically conditioned modes of understanding and expression. Or, again, one may place at the centre of the pattern, not the classical origins of Quakerism nor its historical mutations, but a broad and comprehensive estimate of the contemporary religious situation and its probable future developments, and then proceed to assess the contribution which a critically assessed but faithfully practised Quakerism might be expected to make in this context.

It seems to me that each of these three approaches expresses a true and important insight, but that the truth of each requires the complementary truths emphasised by the other two. However difficult it may be to do so, I therefore want to try to give their due place to all three approaches, and to develop an understanding of the Quaker identity which is influenced by them all. My own reading of the evidence points strongly to a conclusion which it will be the main purpose of the remainder of this chapter to spell out, and to draw the consequences which follow from it for our understanding of ourselves and of our task in the world today.

Two Convergent Lines

I believe the way forward for Quakerism is indicated by two convergent lines of evidence. The first line involves our recognition of two facts. One is that the original thrust of Quakerism was towards the expression of a comprehensive interpretation of the nature, relationships and destiny of man as these are illuminated by the total fact of Jesus recognised as the Christ, the focal and definitive expression of what is ultimately real. In other words, it involves our recognition of the fact that original Quakerism was centred in Jesus Christ as the decisive revelation, in concrete, historical and personal terms, of God.

64

This may be expressed in theological shorthand by saying that original Quakerism was Christo-centric.[82] The second fact, intimately involved with this, is that original Quakerism was radical, for it was concerned to draw out from this Christ-centredness implications which were fresh and daring, and to apply these in uncompromising fashion to whole areas of life which had been generally insulated from them by custom and convention. These two facts together justify us, I believe, in expressing the original vision of Quakerism as a radical Christ-centredness or a Christ-centred radicalism.[83]

The second line of evidence involves the recognition that these same phrases could be appropriately employed to describe the underlying, sometimes unconscious and often equivocally expressed thrust of what is positive in the new Reformation movement. In other words, what gives this whole trend or tendency in contemporary religion and theology such unity and importance as it possesses is its recognition that the knowledge which is available to us of what is ultimately real and significant is to be defined and assessed in terms of what is given in the person of Jesus. Furthermore, this insight finds characteristic expression, not in attempts to construct large and comprehensive theological and philosophical systems, but in radical concern to challenge the existing social, political and economic order, to witness against injustice and oppression and to give practical and organised expression to compassion. It is closely allied, also, with radical criticism of many aspects of the inherited and traditional features of religion, both in doctrine and in institutions. In both respects, therefore, it reproduces

[82] The evidence for this statement is set out in some detail in my *Early Quaker Christology*; unpublished Ph.D. Thesis; University of Leeds 1956; copy in Library of the Society of Friends, London; also available on Microfilm.

[83] cf. Dr. J. J. Vincent's use of the phrase 'Christo-centric radicalism' to define his own position in *Here I Stand: the Faith of a Radical*. London: Epworth, 1967, pp. 22-8.

several important features of the original Quaker attitude.

I have called these two lines of evidence 'convergent'. By this I mean that, unless I am altogether mistaken, the vision and experience to which Quakerism in its origins gave corporate expression is a vision and an experience which is again, in our day, haunting and disquieting and inspiring men and women of all churches and of none. The course on which the Society began originally to move, and the course on which many of the more sensitive and responsible of our contemporaries are feeling their way forward are courses which could bring about a meeting which, I am persuaded, may be of decisive significance for both. To change the metaphor, it may be said that those who have truly heard the message of early Friends and those who are open to the positive message of the new Reformation are 'on the same wavelength', and should be able to communicate without too much difficulty and to their mutual profit. In so far as Friends see this to be so and are prepared to enter into serious dialogue of this kind, I believe we shall be delivered from our 'aimlessness'. To say this is to recognise that, at the present time, the Society of Friends has an opportunity to speak to the condition of its contemporaries in a way it has not had since the seventeenth century. There is, I believe, an openness to what we are justified by our historical experience and tradition in saying. An open door has been set before us. It would be tragic indeed if we failed to perceive it. It would be no less tragic if, perceiving it, we thought that what was required of us was nothing more than either a conventional clinging to seventeenth-century expressions and attitudes, or an accommodation on our part with the traditional attitudes of either Protestant or Catholic piety, or even the abandonment of any kind of commitment to a corporate witness and the justification of this attitude in the name of 'religious freedom' or 'openness to truth'.

Christ-centred Radicalism

I turn now to an attempt to define more explicitly what I mean by the phrase 'Christ-centred radicalism'. I do so, realising that the term 'Christo-centric' or 'Christ-centred' has become for many Friends a kind of shibboleth.[84] It is used—or rejected—in ways which contribute to misunderstanding and divisiveness, and it might therefore be thought wiser to abandon it. But I believe our proper course is to rehabilitate it, for it points, as no other word can do, when rightly understood, to something quite essential to Quakerism.

First of all, I note that the phrase *Christ-centred radicalism* brings together the two dimensions which, as Friends have always rightly insisted, must never be separated—the dimension of insight and faith and that of practical expression in life. Quakers are radicals in that they have always tried to get down beneath appearances, to penetrate to the roots, and to propose remedies not for the symptoms but for the causes of human disorder and distress. But the inspiration and justification of this radical concern have always been derived from that understanding of the human condition and that resource of spiritual power for its remedying and redemption which are supremely expressed and embodied in Jesus Christ.

But these words are rightly used to describe the essence of Quakerism for another reason. Friends are radically Christ-centred in the sense that their understanding of Jesus Christ has radically determined their understanding of both God and man. Early Friends rightly reproached many of their contemporaries for employing conceptions of God which were practically uninfluenced by their beliefs concerning Christ. Most Puritans, for example, appeared to accept the idea of an inflexibly 'just' Father who requires to be 'satisfied' by the self-sacrifice of a compassionate Son. Friends insisted that

[84] *Judges*, xii, 6.

what Christ was historically God is eternally, that, as Paul knew, it is *God* who, in Christ, is reconciling the world to himself.[85] In this they were certainly true to the New Testament and to a central tradition of Christian theology. Similarly, early Friends took with radical seriousness another central emphasis of the Christian tradition when, by their insistence that 'every man is enlightened by the divine light of Christ', they showed their determination to place at the centre of their conception of man not simply the 'first Adam', fallen, degenerate and dead, but that of the 'last Adam', Jesus Christ. This, they said, is what man essentially is in the purpose of God. His actual state of alienation is a tragic fact, but it is to the divine resources for overcoming this state, in Christ, that they looked for their determinative conception of man. In every man, therefore, they saw, not simply the actual, empirical facts of his present state, but also the Christ in him, the divine idea or image of man which was in him struggling to be born, and to the 'answering' of which they directed all their energies.

The same concentration upon Christ was the inspiration of the early Quaker critique of the church, its ministry, its worship and its institutional forms. Their starting point in relation to all these matters was expressed in the phrase 'Christ has come to teach his people himself'. He alone is the Prophet, to whose words we must attend; he is the sole Priest, upon whose mediation we depend; his Kingship neither requires nor brooks any structures of continuity or authority modelled upon those of earthly rule.

It should not be necessary to labour the point that in some respects these characteristic emphases of Quakerism bear a significant resemblance to those of some of the most influential exponents of the insights and attitudes which underlie the new Reformation. Such Christ-centredness is the source of the

[85] 2 *Corinthians*, v, 19.

power of a Bonhoeffer to haunt us with his insistent question 'Who, and what, is Christ for us today?'; it is also the secret of his power (whatever reservations we may feel about the decision to which it led him), to take responsibility for radical political involvement, to witness to Christ with patience and fortitude throughout a long imprisonment and finally to seal his discipleship in the joyful acceptance of death. Such Christ-centredness is also the inspiration and organising principle of the vast panorama of cosmic evolution unfolded by a Teilhard de Chardin.

Nor should it be necessary to point out that it is a complete misunderstanding of the meaning of Christ-centredness to regard it as involving a narrow and exclusive outlook, or to oppose it to a 'theocentric' emphasis. To be Christo-centric is not to concentrate upon Christ as over against or in preference to God; but it is to recognise that the only meaning of the word God which is worth discussing is the meaning which Jesus gave it. It is to realise that it is the grace of our Lord Jesus Christ which opens our eyes and our hearts to the love of God and draws us into the fellowship of the Holy Spirit. It is to perceive that it is when the Word becomes flesh that we are given grounds for trusting that the grace and truth there revealed have been in and with God from the beginning, that they are the light which enlightens every man, and that even where this light is unrecognised, the darkness does not overwhelm it. Christ-centredness is the inevitable consequence of our recognition that the Word is defined by, though not confined to, Jesus.[86] Perhaps John Macquarrie has said most memorably what needs to be said on this point when he speaks of the event of Jesus Christ as 'symbol' and as 'focus'. It

[86] As John Robinson has said (*Honest to God*, p. 73) Jesus, while not claiming to be God personally, nevertheless does claim to bring God completely. Cf. N. Pittenger in *The Word Incarnate*. London: Nisbet, 1959, *passim*.

focuses, he says, 'the presence and activity which are indeed everywhere, but of which we remain unaware until such a focusing occurs, and the "mystery hidden for ages" is made "manifest". Jesus Christ then is the focus where the mystery of Being is disclosed'.[87]

To claim all this is not to be blind to the sad fact that there has been and still is a 'Christ-centredness' which is indeed narrow, individualistic and sterile. This may take the form of an ultra-evangelicalism which appears to ignore every manifestation of God's unitive, reconciling and gracious presence except that which can be comprehended within a precisely defined conversion experience in which Christ becomes simply 'my personal Saviour'. Or it may take a form which might more properly be called 'Jesus-centredness', combining a rejection of the interpretation of Jesus given by the central Christian tradition with a sometimes uncritical and even sentimental devotion to Jesus, whether as the great exemplar, supreme ethical teacher, religious genius or social revolutionary.

The interpretation which I have been giving of Christ-centredness is, I believe, claiming no more—and, I hope, no less—than is claimed throughout the New Testament as a whole. It is to proclaim, with Paul, 'the good news of the unfathomable riches of Christ', and to speak of the purpose which 'was hidden for long ages in God the creator of the universe' and which was eventually 'achieved in Christ Jesus our Lord', with the consequence that 'in him we have access to God with freedom, in the confidence born of trust in him'.[88] It is 'to come to the full wealth of conviction which understanding brings'; it is to 'grasp God's secret', which is 'Christ himself',

---

[87] See John Macquarrie's *Principles of Christian Theology*. London: SCM, 1966, p. 249; also *Christ for us Today*; papers from the Fiftieth Annual Conference of Modern Churchmen, ed. N. Pittenger. London: SCM, 1967, *passim*.

[88] *Ephesians*, iii, 8 f.

in whom 'lie hidden all God's treasures of wisdom and know-ledge'.[89] For it was 'through him God chose to reconcile the whole universe to himself'.[90]

And this interpretation is, I no less firmly believe, in harmony with the original witness of Friends, on almost every page of whose writings passages such as these I have quoted lie thickly scattered. And they are there because early Friends knew that, as they became obedient to the inward promptings of love and truth, interpreted in the light of such passages as the promptings of the spirit of Christ within them, they expressed a truth of their own experience. They saw that the divine purpose was one of liberation and reconciliation involving all men and even the whole creation. They knew that, central and decisive in the effecting of this purpose was the life, death and resurrection of Jesus Christ; and they knew that, in proportion as they yielded themselves up to the mysterious yet most real continuing presence of Christ in their own lives and in the 'silent assem-blies of God's people', they were given deeper insight into the mystery of that presence and were enabled more and more to become its committed servants.

This was the Christ-centred radicalism of the New Testa-ment and of seventeenth-century Quakerism. And this, I am persuaded, when all allowances have been made for the use of different language, for whatever 'de-mythologizing' may justifi-ably be required, is the inner core of conviction which gives the new Reformation movement in our own day whatever direction and dynamism it possesses. And both classical Quakerism and the contemporary radical theology agree in recognising that the words men use to express their understanding of the mystery of Christ are of less significance than their willingness to place themselves under his yoke.

[89] *Colossians*, ii, 2-4.
[90] *Colossians*, i, 20.

The Tendency Towards 'Polarisation'

I want now to look at some of the implications and consequences of the argument I have been developing for a fuller
understanding of some important aspects of our life as a
religious Society. Some of these mainly involve fresh interpretation and understanding of well-known features of that life;
others involve the need for decisions in the field of practical
action, both in the internal life of the Society and also in its
external relationships.

I wish to suggest that the view I have put forward of the
essential nature of Quakerism as a radical Christ-centredness,
or a Christ-centred radicalism, provides a perspective from
which we can gain a clearer understanding of the Society's
history than is afforded by some other more widely entertained
views. It throws some light, also, upon the divisions within the
Society, and, consequently, upon the conditions upon which
they may be healed.

It may be generally agreed that, in the nineteenth and
twentieth centuries the Society of Friends has tended to become
polarised into two parts. The names or labels which are used to
denote these vary a good deal, and the groupings thus variously
indicated are by no means identical. But the broad fact of such
a polarisation into an 'evangelical' and a 'liberal' wing is not,
I think, in question. Following the description of the essence of
Quakerism which I have given earlier in this chapter, I should
be inclined to employ another pair of labels, and to say that a
large part of the Society is 'Christ-centred' but not noticeably
'radical' while another part is 'radical' but not noticeably
'Christ-centred'. By Christ-centred, in this connection, I mean
standing firmly in the main orthodox Christian tradition,
emphasising the importance of such matters as conversion,
evangelisation and holiness. By radical I mean concerned to
give priority to individual and corporate action in the interests

of such causes as civil rights, relief of sufferings, and protest movements of various kinds in the cause of peace and reconciliation.

These are, of course, very rough and ready terms, and I do not claim for them greater accuracy than I would accord to the remark of an American Friend of my acquaintance to the effect that some Friends in his country were Christians but not Quakers, whereas others were Quakers but not Christians. But the point I am concerned to make is, I hope, sufficiently clear. By whatever terms we describe them, there appear to be two components or emphases within Quakerism which are in tension, and that, in any given area of the Society, the prevailing component gives its character to the Society's internal life, attitudes and relationships. But it seems very clear to the Friends of one type that the Quakerism of Friends of the other is, on the whole, defective, even though they may recognise in it, however imperfectly expressed, values which their own type of Quakerism lacks or does not sufficiently appreciate.

An Unresolved Tension

The question I wish to raise is this; whence comes this polarity and tension, the consequences of which are written so clearly across the Society's history? The answer to this question is not to be found, I believe, in the external influences which at different times and in various places have played upon the Society. Nor is it supplied by talk about the balance existing at any given time among the various emphases such as the 'prophetic', the 'mystical' and the 'humanitarian' which are held to be inherent in Quakerism. Such talk describes but does not explain. The answer is to be found, I am maintaining, in an unresolved tension deep within the Quakerism of the seventeenth century. To recognise and understand the nature of this tension is, I believe, to be well on the way to an under-

73

standing of what is called for if the consequent divisions are to be overcome, so that the Society can make once again a united witness.

Of course, in one sense, tension between faith and practice, between belief and action, between preoccupation with the demands of the outward life and the cultivation of the inward life, is inherent in Christianity, which will not tolerate for long the sacrifice of either to the other, nor allow either to be dealt with in isolation from the other. But in the case of Quakerism, this subtle and complex relationship was made more difficult of achievement by the circumstances of its origin. The original concern of Quakerism can be described in terms of *a contrast* and *an emphasis*. It sought to drive home to its contemporaries the *contrast* between on the one hand a genuine, radical transforming openness and obedience to the living spirit of Christ encountered in the life of the present moment, in oneself and in others, and on the other, a merely formal and conventional acquiescence in the beliefs and practices of traditional Christianity. These beliefs and practices might, indeed, be true and good in themselves; but they all could so easily be held and practised 'out of the life' or 'notionally'. This contrast was, at the beginning, expressed by such terms as 'inward', meaning genuine, and 'outward' meaning formal or notional. Early Quakerism sought, furthermore, to place the greatest possible *emphasis* upon the contemporary and universal aspects of the significance of Jesus Christ, and they expressed this emphasis characteristically in such phrases as 'the divine and universal light of Christ', 'the Christ within' or 'that of God in every man'.

But even before the end of the seventeenth century, these terms had changed their meaning, or had come to be used in senses which were distinguishable from their original intention. Thus 'inward' came to mean 'immediate' in the sense of unmediated; and 'outward' came to mean 'historical' or mediated by the senses or natural faculties.[91] Similarly, 'the light' came to be understood and interpreted as in some sense independent of, or even as an advance upon, the historic Christ.

My contention is that the predisposing cause of the tendency already referred to towards bifurcation or polarisation in the Quaker tradition, is the tension between what I may call the content and the form of early Quakerism. Its content was, I am convinced, intensely Christ-centred, deeply rooted in the whole Hebrew-Biblical-Christian faith and experience. But, due to the circumstances of the origins of Quakerism in seventeenth-century England, this content was expressed in the form of an inner-light doctrine which, despite the sincere and strenuous protestations of the Quaker publicists, was understood by their contemporaries as disparaging the historic Christ, minimising the reality of man's need to be taught the Christian tradition, and denigrating the intellect and the premeditated as contrasted with the ecstatic and the extempore.[92]

Our History Interpreted

It is from this perspective, I believe, that the Quietist phase of the Society's history is to be understood, although, of course, external influences and the spirit of the age were also predisposing and contributory causes. During this period, it would not be altogether unfair to say, the Society generally ceased to be Christ-centred and also ceased to be Radical. It entered upon a period of something like suspended animation,

[91] For a fuller discussion, see my *'Inward' and 'Outward'; a Study in Early Quaker Language.* Friends Hist. Soc. supl. 30. London: Friends Historical Society, 1962.
[92] For a fuller treatment, see my *The Christ of History and of Experience.* Seventh Shrewsbury Lecture, August 1967, given at Friends Meeting House, Shrewsbury, New Jersey, U.S.A. (Available from Friends Book Centre, Friends House, Euston Road, N.W.1.)

6

concentrating its energies upon preserving itself as a 'peculiar people', no longer able—or even desirous—of speaking to the condition either of the 'cultivated despisers' of religion or of the new near-pagan proletariat produced by the agrarian and industrial revolution.

The tides of spiritual renewal flowed into eighteenth-century England through Methodism, not through Quakerism. But soon these tides made their presence felt in the Society. Harnessed as they were within a pronounced Evangelicalism, and flowing into a socially privileged and inbred Society, their undoubted Christ-centredness did not produce the radical effects which accompanied the Quaker apprehension of Christ in the previous century. Instead, they encouraged the Society to accept the role of an evangelical Protestant denomination, neither radically challenging nor radically challenged by other evangelical groups. Nevertheless, the recovery of Christ-centredness, even in this restricted form, soon began to find expression in humanitarian and social terms, even if not in particularly radical forms and not always free from patronising or paternalistic overtones. But it is more than a coincidence that Elizabeth Fry, Joseph John Gurney and William Allen, to name only three of the Friends of this period whose work and influence decisively established the Quaker image which is still widely accepted, were Friends in whom Christ-centredness and powerful social concern were inextricably involved.

Due to the close and frequent communication maintained between Friends on both sides of the Atlantic, similar developments took place among Friends in America. The British Friends whose prestige and authority carried most weight there were Friends whose Quakerism was Christ-centred in the sense and within the qualifications I have just indicated. Their influence served to concentrate attention upon the inner tension between content and form which I have noted as having been present in Quakerism from the beginning. Under pioneer conditions, and in the absence of the firm and close social environment and sense of tradition characteristic of British Quakerism, this tension was heightened to such an extent that it broke the spiritual unity of the Society in America, and found institutional expression in separate and parallel series of Yearly Meetings, until recently out of fellowship with one another. While there were, of course, non-theological factors at work in this situation such as the inevitable tensions between an urban membership of some wealth and sophistication on the one hand, and a rural membership conscious of its limitations on the other, the separations were primarily on theological lines. Over against a rather cool and sometimes complacent acceptance of the inherited attitudes of the Quietist period of Quakerism, there came into being a fervent but often narrow and intolerant emphasis upon the traditional but limited Christ-centredness of evangelical piety.

During the last thirty years, and notably through the work of the Friends World Committee for Consultation, the series of World Conferences of Friends and the publications of the Quaker Theological Discussion Group,[93] these and related differences among Friends have been faced with growing knowledge and much genuine mutual appreciation. All this suggests great cause for thankfulness. But if all that is at work here could be shown to be a mere kindly tolerance not unconnected with indifference; or, more positively, a pluralism which simply rejoices in diversities for their own sake, I do not believe that these developments give grounds for great optimism for the future of Quakerism. But this open and appreciative attitude can, I believe, provide the indispensable setting for a concerted and co-operative effort of an intellectual and, indeed, profoundly religious and theological kind, leading

[93] For details see Suggestions for further reading on page 89.

towards the emergence of a Quakerism appropriate to the twenty-first century.

An Internal and External Dialogue

The time is ripe, I believe, for the Society to engage as never before in both an internal and an external dialogue. Both must proceed together, although our ability to sustain an effective external dialogue depends in a measure upon how far we will have been able to reach a greater internal consensus. To take first the internal dialogue, I have been trying in this chapter to suggest perspectives which may help us to understand why it is that, in the Society as a whole, throughout the world, Friends have tended to cluster themselves, if I may employ diagrammatic terms, around the centres of two circles, finding it possible, within each group, to converse among themselves with ease and enjoyment. Among the members of one group an imaginary eavesdropper would be likely to overhear frequent references to Christ, the Holy Spirit, Salvation, the Scriptures, Evangelism and Prayer. Among the members of the other group he would be more likely to hear references to God as known in 'mystical experience', to 'openness to truth', to 'seekers', meditation, testimonies and service.

In the past—thankfully, much less in the present—he might have overheard, tossed between the two groups, words that sounded like 'creaturely activity', 'other-worldliness' and 'so-called Friends'. But what we today need to understand, and what I believe we are now in a mood to understand, is that the true genius of the Society of Friends requires that the two points around which Friends have for so long tended to rally are not the centres of two distinct, even if partially overlapping, circles, but are, so to speak, the two foci of an ellipse. The true shape of Quakerism can only be traced if it relates all the time at every point to both. The 'Christ-centred' Friend and the 'radical' Friend are to be seen as belonging together, each requiring the other for his own self-understanding, each preventing the other from becoming shallow or complacent and self-sufficient, each in creative tension with the other.[94] Only when we see this to be so shall we be able to respond adequately to the inspiring call which Hugh Doncaster made in his opening address to the Fourth World Conference of Friends at Guilford in 1967, that Friends should involve themselves in 'creative encounter'.

And only in so far as we do this shall we be able, as a Society, to engage effectively in what I have called the external dialogue, and, in particular, with those groups and individuals who are seeking to express the positive insights of what we have been calling the new Reformation. For what the new Reformation brings home to us is the fact that our internal dialogue is being carried on in the presence of the vast, unseen audience of our contemporaries to whom most of what is said on both sides is either meaningless or irrelevant. For them, our two groups are already united—in a common incomprehensibility—and are therefore dismissed with an impartial indifference. But the new Reformation is also calling upon us to recognise the immense needs of our contemporaries for a sense of meaning and purpose in their lives, so that they may apply themselves, free from a sense of ultimate futility, to such vast problems as the growing imbalance between population and natural resources, the attainment by the rapidly developing countries of a measure of political maturity and, ever in the background, the maintenance in peace of a stable world order.

But the new Reformation is not only challenging us to face this vast panorama of human needs. In the hands of its pro-

[94] See my essay in *The Creative Centre of Quakerism* (being papers read at the 9th meeting of FWCC) ed. Kenneth L. Carroll. Birmingham: Friends World Committee for Consultation, 1965.

founder exponents it is challenging all Christians to take with a new and more radical seriousness the original Christian claim that it is in the face of the man Jesus that the 'glory' of God is to be seen, that it is Jesus Christ who is the 'stamp of God's very being',[95] that what is to be known of God is to be learned from him, and that God is to be served only in so far as he is discerned and ministered to in the persons of Christ's brethren.[96] All this and much more the new Reformation is saying to us. What can and should we be able to say in response?

Our Response to the new Reformation

In so far as we are led towards a genuine consensus of the kind I have indicated by the terms Christ-centred radicalism or radical Christ-centredness, I believe there are several very relevant and important things we shall be entitled to say. We shall be entitled, for example, to say that the Society of which we are members can testify, out of an experience of more than three centuries, that it is possible for men and women to find meaning, purpose, deliverance from anxiety, fear and enslavement to convention, and to enter into deep and satisfying relationships and to find true community. We shall affirm that such things have been given to us on the sole condition of our willingness to be gathered in obedience to 'the Presence in the midst', which we understand to be the Presence promised by Jesus, whether we describe it, with Paul, as 'God's Spirit', 'the Spirit of Christ', 'Christ' or 'the Spirit of him who raised Christ Jesus from the dead',[97] or even find it necessary to use quite other terms. Furthermore, we can say that, in order to know this experience, we do not find it essential to depend upon the ministrations of any specially ordained persons, or to

[95] *Hebrews*, i. 3.
[96] *Matthew*, xxv, 31-46.
[97] *Romans*, viii, 9-10.

follow any prescribed liturgical patterns of worship. But we do find it essential to look for and to relate ourselves to the Christ who is to be encountered in every man, who is to be ministered to in every situation of need, suffering, deprivation or injustice. Again, we do not find it necessary to insist upon the acceptance of precise credal statements as a pre-condition of knowing this experience, although we do find ourselves constrained to acknowledge unreservedly our need to be 'humble learners in the school of Christ', with our 'faces towards the light'.

The implications which the existence of such a Society has for the new Reformation movement are, it seems to me, plain and momentous. It demonstrates the viability of a religious fellowship without the hierarchical, ecclesiastical and institutional features which are so prominent in the Roman, Orthodox and main-line Protestant churches and which, to many people today, seem such hindrances to those churches' ability to relate themselves creatively to one another and to the modern world. It exhibits the possibility, under modern conditions, of the combination of profoundly religious concern with genuine intellectual openness and freedom, of a refusal to recognise any ultimate divorce between the sacred and the secular. It shows, too, that a high degree of ethical sensitiveness and responsibility can exist in the almost complete absence of a legalistic or prescriptive moral code. Admittedly, if the Society had been more alert than it has been to the danger of erecting its experience of the non-necessity of hierarchy, liturgy, creed, sacrament and professional ministry into a rigid insistence on the necessity of not recognising in any circumstances any value in these things, it would have had greater justification for such claims. Furthermore, the Society has never, I think, faced with sufficient frankness the possibility that some of its most highly prized freedoms may be as much the consequences of its small size, social homogeneity and relatively high economic and educational level as of its religious insights. And Quakerism, it must be admitted, has not yet provided convincing evidence of its ability to meet the spiritual needs of all sorts and conditions of men, though this is not to say that it cannot do so if it takes its central affirmation of the 'freeness and spirituality of the gospel' with greater seriousness and radicalness than it has yet done.

Some Practical Consequences for Ourselves

But such a consensus would not only justify us in making the kind of contribution I have been describing. It would also entail our making a number of practical decisions and choices concerning both the Society's internal life and its external relationships. It would affect, for example, our approach to *outreach or extension work* and our understanding of the *meaning of membership*. Are we to exhibit to enquirers simply the image of an open religious association which, we might claim, possesses most of the features they naturally find attractive, has none, or few, of those which put them off other churches, and which makes few demands upon individual freedom either of belief or of practice? Or are we to invite them to enter into a fellowship committed corporately to a specific vision and task, and to say to them 'If there is something in you which responds to this, then perhaps your rightful place is with us'? And do we make it clear to any who apply for membership in the Society that they are seeking to join a Society which corporately intends to embody and witness to a specific interpretation of the meaning and purpose of life, and that this has as its creative centre and focus a corporate insight into the significance and a corporate loyalty to the person and way of Jesus Christ? We should not, indeed insist that every member must accept any given verbal formulation of this insight and loyalty. But we ought, I believe, to leave him in no doubt that this is the corporate commitment of the Society he is seeking to join, and that, in joining it, he will be placing himself under a corporate care and discipline the aim of which is to draw all of us into an ever fuller vision while leaving each of us free to express in his own way what loyalty to that vision means to him.

Again, to accept such a view of the essential nature of the Society commits us, I believe, to a greatly enhanced recognition of the importance of ministry. If we have been right to reject clericalism, as I firmly believe we have been, it is not so clear that we have always distinguished between this and the recognition of a genuine vocation to ministry. The mere absence of a trained and professional ministry, unless it opens the way to a deep and serious concern for the recognition, encouragement and support of vocation to ministry, wherever it may appear among the members, is a feature of only negative importance. If the Society is rightly understood as corporately committed to a radical Christ-centredness, then it needs today, at least as much as it did in its beginnings, men and women who will give first priority in time and strength to the work of ministry, involving serious teaching and learning in groups for worship, study and discussion. If such were forthcoming, modern conditions of mobility would make possible a re-creation of something like the itinerant ministry which was the lifeblood of the early Quaker movement. It is towards some such conception of ministry that many in other traditions are feeling their way; and our own conception and experience, interpreted in relation to the contemporary situation, could give to us the possibility of demonstrating its continuing validity.

It is, finally, in the areas of ecumenical and inter-faith relationships that the reapprehension of our original radically Christ-centred vision can be seen as involving significant choices and decisions. In the first place, it means that we cannot think of ourselves as detached from or indifferent to the efforts of the churches to come into some more obvious expression of their unity, particularly as that unity is ever more clearly seen by them as constituted by their common relation to Christ. But, as I pointed out in the previous chapter, the ecumenical movement itself has given rise to a heightened awareness among the churches that history has occasioned the emergence of several distinguishable understandings of the church, and that the crucial issue of the movement concerns the right understanding of their relationship. By their recognition of the Society of Friends as 'a standing perplexity', churchmen of different traditions give expression to their sense both of the significance and of the distinctiveness of the Quaker interpretation of the church. We have an obligation, I believe, to take ourselves in this respect with at least as much seriousness as that with which they take us, and to play our full part in the ecumenical dialogue. This should be all the more obvious to us, I suggest, when we recognise that the ecumenical movement expressed in both world and national councils of churches, and notably at the Fourth Assembly of the World Council of Churches at Uppsala last year, is showing an increasingly active and informed concern with the great social, economic and international problems of the world, and with the church's responsibilities in relation to them. This is, of course, but one aspect of the church's growing awareness of the profound and mysterious sense in which the presence of Christ is to be discerned and his purposes to be served in the secular affairs of men, an insight to which Friends have ever been open. And the ecumenical dialogue is also coming to be increasingly concerned with responding to the presence of Christ in the non-Christian religions, and with the implications of this for the mission of the church in the world, another aspect of something which has been central in the Society's outlook from the beginning.

'Narrow' or 'Exclusive'?

It may be, however, that, regarding all that I have said about the consequences of our accepting the role of expressing a radical Christ-centredness, some Friends may feel uneasy about what they may still think of as a 'narrowing' or an 'exclusiveness' inseparable from this position. Let me therefore admit that there is indeed a sense in which these words may be properly applicable to what I have said. There is an exclusiveness and a narrowing involved. It is the exclusiveness and narrowing of the artist's eye, which, amidst all the multiplicity of detail, seizes and concentrates upon the form which gives meaning, coherence and unity to all the rest. It is the narrowing of attention of the musician's ear, trained to discern the basic themes of a composition, and to attend to other sounds only in so far as they anticipate, reinforce, modify or echo those themes. It is the narrowing which is involved in any man's acceptance of the need to concentrate upon acquiring a skill or fulfilling an obligation. It is the exclusiveness of the man who, forsaking all others, cleaves only to his wife. But, as expressions of a paradox which is surely familiar to everyone, such narrowing or exclusiveness is the inescapable condition of understanding, of appreciation, of knowledge and of enriching relationships. It is the paradox of 'whose service is perfect freedom', of 'make me a captive, Lord, and then I shall be free'. And, if we must hear it in Quaker phrases, it is the paradox expressed in Isaac Penington's words: 'The perfection of the true liberty lies in the perfection of bonds; in the perfect binding down of that which is out of the life.'[98]

[98] Penington (Isaac) An Exhortation to the Present Age, *Works* I, p. 131, 1681 edition.

Quakerism is most truly understood, I believe, as an interpretation of the central meaning of the Christian gospel. If I may again use an analogy from music, I take the sole task of the interpreter to be the setting forth of the inner richness and beauty of the music he is performing, bringing out all the depth and subtlety of the musical creation. The greatness of the interpreter is measured by two criteria; has he devoted himself wholeheartedly to the task of penetrating into the composer's mind? And does he do this with complete self-forgetfulness; concerned to say not 'Listen to me interpreting Beethoven' but only 'Listen to Beethoven'? The value of the Quaker interpretation of the unsearchable riches of Christ is to be measured, I believe, by the same criteria, calling for the same dedication and the same humility.

A Personal Conclusion

I began this lecture by speaking very personally about the questions which press themselves upon a Friend who both desires to respond positively and with genuine openness to the contemporary world and who also knows that in Jesus Christ he has been 'convinced of Truth'. Now, as I come to its end, I want to summarise no less personally, and as honestly as I know how, the conclusions towards which the considerations suggested in this lecture seem to me persuasively to point.

I believe the ferment of questioning of religious beliefs, practices and structures which I have been calling the new Reformation is to be welcomed, expressing as it does a response to the truly overwhelming expansion of knowledge, power and responsibility which has taken place with ever accelerating pace during the past three centuries. This response, because it is human, is mixed and ambiguous, and gives occasion for the expression of impatience, resentment, partiality and pride. Despite all this, I believe there is also ex-

86

pressed in it a genuine desire to know both what is true and also what we ought to do. There is evidence that its more sensational and negative features have been transitory exaggerations, and that, through it, many people are rediscovering the challenge of authentic faith and the bracing demand of moral commitment. 'Christendom' and a legally or culturally 'established Christianity' are now coming to be seen for the fictions and distortions which, in large part, they have always been. There is, therefore, a greater readiness now than for centuries past, among members of many churches, to recognise that being a Christian requires an intention of discipleship and that only in so far as they lead to discipleship have religious experience or orthodoxy of belief or sacramental incorporation any meaning, or ministerial and pastoral functions any authority. The church is therefore coming increasingly to be seen, not simply as human society in its religious aspect, nor as an 'ark of salvation', but as the intentional community within which the meaning for the present day of the appearance of Jesus Christ is constantly contemplated, celebrated and explored, and which, through the forming of 'the mind of Christ' within the individual members, is corporately committed to obedience at the present time to the divine purpose which he embodied.

If I am right in understanding the positive thrust of the new Reformation in some such terms as these, I believe I am also justified in claiming that the Quaker understanding of Christian faith and practice is significantly similar to it. From this fact I do not draw the conclusion that Quakerism no longer has any distinctive role to play. Rather, I see Quakerism as having a greater opportunity at the present time of speaking to the condition of contemporary men and women than it has ever had since the seventeenth century. It can do this, not only because it understands and sympathises with much in their mood of radical questioning, search and protest, but also because it knows, in its corporate experience over three centuries, the reality of a presence and a power which focuses, to their mutual enrichment and harmony, the experience of worship, community and service, and thus 'answers that of God in every man'.

But if the justification of such high claims for Quakerism is its embodiment of what I have been calling radical Christ-centredness, this same Christ-centred radicalism is the standard before which not a little of the Society's history and present condition lies under judgement. We have allowed a whole gospel to decline into something perilously like a half-truth; we have only half-heartedly accepted the disciplines and obligations implicit in our original insights; and we have only timidly attempted the task of expressing our message and our corporate life in language, practices and forms which are genuinely related to the present day.

Yet I firmly believe that the Society of Friends throughout the world is being called at this time to a renewed commitment to its original insight that the reality of both God and man is disclosed in Jesus Christ and that man's freedom and fulfilment are to be found in obedience to the way of Christ, learned in a worshipping fellowship informed by his spirit. And I believe no less firmly that, if we will be obedient at this time to this vision, the days of our greatest witness and service lie before us.

Suggestions for further reading

A. Two books which provide respectively a comprehensive survey of 'the frontiers of philosophy and theology 1900-1960' and an attempt to express the Christian faith 'in terms that communicate with the secular culture of our time'.

John Macquarrie: *Twentieth-Century Religious Thought*. London: SCM Press, 1963
John Macquarrie: *Principles of Christian Theology*. London: SCM Press, 1966

B. Four Series of books which deal in lucid and stimulating ways with most aspects of contemporary Christian thinking.
The New Reformation Series: published by Epworth Press
The Directions in Theology Today: published by Lutterworth Press
SCM Centrebooks: published by SCM Press
Fontana Books: published by Collins

C. The most significant Quaker thinking on these and related matters is to be found in *Quaker Religious Thought*, published twice yearly, and obtainable from The Circulation Manager, *Quaker Religious Thought*, Rio Grande College, Rio Grande, Ohio 45674, U.S.A., or from Woodbrooke, 1046 Bristol Road, Selly Oak, Birmingham 29.

THE SWARTHMORE LECTURES

The following lectures have been reprinted in the Swarthmore Lecture Pamphlet series.

Several of the Lectures earlier than 1949 are still in print and a complete list will be sent on request to the Friends Home Service Committee, Friends House, Euston Road, London N.W.1.

30.